When Morning Gilds the Skies

Great Hymns of Our Faith

BOOK 1:

O Worship the King

BOOK 2:

O Come, All Ye Faithful

BOOK 3:

What Wondrous Love Is This

BOOK 4:

When Morning Gilds the Skies

Hymns of Heaven and Our Eternal Hope

When Morning Gilds the Skies

JONI EARECKSON TADA

JOHN MACARTHUR

ROBERT & BOBBIE WOLGEMUTH

CROSSWAY BOOKS • WHEATON, ILLINOIS

A DIVISION OF GOOD NEWS PUBLISHERS

When Morning Gilds the Skies

Published by Crossway Books
A division of Good News Publishers
1300 Crescent Street
Wheaton, Illinois 60187

Design: Cindy Kiple

First printing: 2002

Printed in the United States of America

ISBN 1-58134-428-7 Book and CD set (sold only as a set)

LIBRARY OF CONGRESS CATALOGING-IN-PUBLICATION DATA
When morning glids the skies : hymns of heaven and our eternal hope /
John MacArthur, Joni Eareckson Tada.
p. cm. — (Great hymns of our faith ; bk. 4)
ISBN 1-58134-428-7 (HC : alk. paper)
1. Hymns, English—History and criticism. I. Tada, Joni Eareckson. II. Title.
III. Series.
BV315 .M35 2002
264'.23—dc21 2002005557
CIP

15 14 13 12 11 10 09 08 07 06 05 04 03 02
15 14 13 12 11 10 9 8 7 6 5 4 3 2 1

To Clayton Erb,
for his music leadership at Grace Community Church
for twenty-four years.
His love for the hymns has spread to our entire
congregation and enriched us all.

JOHN MACARTHUR

To my happy harmonizer, Bev Singleton.
Nobody sings a hymn with deeper passion,
a bigger smile, or greater gusto.

JONI EARECKSON TADA

To Grace Wolgemuth
who never stops singing;
our mother, the sweet soprano,
who just ushered our precious father, Samuel, into glory
with hymns of hope and heaven.

ROBERT & BOBBIE WOLGEMUTH

Special Thanks to:

Mr. John Duncan
of TVP Studios, Greenville, SC,
Executive Producer of the musical recording
for *When Morning Gilds the Skies*.

Dr. Paul Plew
Chairman of the Department of Music
at The Master's College,
who directed the musical production.

The students of The Master's Chorale
who contributed their superb singing skills
and love for these hymns to the CD.

We are deeply grateful for the gifts of these friends
and accomplished professionals.

The publisher's share of income from the *When Morning Gilds the Skies* compact disc is being donated by Good News Publishers/Crossway Books to Joni and Friends, the worldwide disability outreach of Joni Eareckson Tada. For more information about Joni and Friends, please write to Joni and Friends, Post Office Box 3333, Agoura Hills, California 91301 or call 818-707-5664 or go to the website—www.joniandfriends.org

---

Table of Contents

FOREWORD

Quite an unusual story lies behind the writing of the books in this series. But then we might expect as much because the authors—Joni Eareckson Tada, John MacArthur, and Robert and Bobbie Wolgemuth—are such extraordinary people!

In the broadest sense this book is the story of God's unfailing faithfulness, as told in the great hymns of the faith and in the stories that lie behind these hymns. Whether written in the midst of overwhelming tragedy or in moments of great joy, the hymns in the books in this series have profoundly touched the lives of Christians through the centuries—and they will do so again as these books are read.

But the immediate story behind this series starts (as many unusual stories do!) with our very dear friend Joni Eareckson Tada. Joni, as you know, broke her neck in a diving accident when she was seventeen years old, and she has lived as a quadriplegic for more than three decades ever since. But by God's grace and through Joni's perseverance, she lives a most extraordinary life—a life that above all else reflects the joy of the Lord. One of my favorite memories, in fact, is stopping with Joni in hotel lobbies to sing impromptu hymns of praise and worship—to the delight and sometimes wonder of other hotel guests.

The occasion that gave birth to this series of books and accompanying CDs, then, was *Joni's* idea—this time to sing "impromptu hymns" with Dr. John MacArthur at the Good News-Crossway 60th Anniversary Banquet, in the summer of 1998. The theme for the banquet was "Celebrating Sixty Years of God's Faithfulness," and both Joni and John MacArthur, Joni's pastor and close friend, were scheduled to speak. Joni and John checked with me first to be sure it was okay—and of course Joni doesn't take "no" for an answer! But it came as a complete surprise to everyone else when Joni invited John to join her on the platform to sing an "impromptu" duet of their favorite hymns.

Rarely have I seen an audience so deeply moved. As they listened to Joni sing the praises of God's faithfulness, it was a remarkable moment—a moment when we were all given a glimpse of God's glory.

Immediately after the banquet I started urging John and Joni to make a CD of hymns. And from there the ideas just kept growing. Joni invited her friends Robert and Bobbie Wolgemuth to join in since, as Joni noted, "We've sung together for years . . . over the telephone, in hotel lobbies, in restaurant parking lots, and they'd love to be part of this." And of course we'd need a book to go with the CD. But there are so many great hymns, we soon realized we'd really need *four* books!

All these ideas have come together in a most exciting way for each book so far. The recording studio was booked; John MacArthur brought Dr. Paul Plew and the highly acclaimed Chorale of The Master's College; and Joni, John, Robert, and Bobbie joined in singing some of the greatest hymns of all time. As Joni reflected after recording the CD for the first book, *O Worship the King*, "The adventure of singing together was pure delight. It was two solid days of worship and praise."

Now, several years after Joni "cooked up" her idea for a duet, her idea continues to come to life in the books in this series and in the CDs tucked into the back covers. It is our prayer that through these books and CDs you will also see a glimpse of God's glory and discover a deeper understanding of His faithfulness, and that you would join with Joni and John and Robert and Bobbie—and indeed the Church of our Lord Jesus Christ through the centuries—in singing the praises of our Lord and Savior.

When morning gilds the skies, my heart awaking cries:
May Jesus Christ be praised.
Alike at work and prayer to Jesus I repair:
May Jesus Christ be praised.

Lane T. Dennis, Ph.D.
Publisher

Introduction

All glory, laud and honor
To thee, Redeemer, King,
To whom the lips of children,
Made sweet hosannas ring.

It was the early ninth century in France. Emperor Louis I was traveling in a ceremonial procession, riding on horseback. The parade wound through Paris, past the city prison. He heard the voice of an inmate singing this great hymn in the original Latin. The prisoner was Archbishop Theodulph of Orleans, a great lover of art and the author of the hymn. In that moment, at the sound of the music, the monarch was moved from lethargy and indifference to genuine faith. The Emperor, known now by historians as Louis the Pious, immediately ordered the release of the archbishop.

Who can measure the power of a hymn?

David Luken was on his way to the Baltimore airport from his home in Kensington, Maryland. It was 4:30 in the morning, and the rain was pouring down like waves sweeping across the highway. As David accelerated onto the interstate from the entrance ramp, he did not see a huge flatbed truck bearing down on him. The trucker's sudden braking and the slick road forced the eighteen-wheeler into a jackknife.

Together David's car and the truck slid to a merciful stop. David's rearview mirror was ripped from the driver's side door . . . but that was all. There was no other damage, except the emotional trauma of the moment. David slowly pulled his car back onto the road and drove on.

Trying to calm his shaking hands and pounding heart, he impulsively reached to the dash and turned on his radio. It was tuned to a station that carried the Focus on the Family broadcast. Dr. James Dobson had just introduced a hymn from the *O Worship the King* CD that Joni and Bobbie were singing.

What language shall I borrow
To thank thee, dearest Friend . . .
Lord, let me never, never
Outlive my love to thee.

The words blanketed David's troubled heart, bringing comfort and solace. "I am not a religious man," he later wrote. "But the beauty of this music convinced me that there must be a living God somewhere."

An uncommon peace swept over David.

Who can measure the power of a hymn?

In the spring of 2000 the four of us met together for the first time to talk about this hymn series. We were meeting around the conference table at the headquarters of Joni & Friends Ministries in Southern California. Our good friends Dr. Lane Dennis and Marvin Padgett from Crossway Books were there to help us narrow down our favorite hymns to the top twelve.

Robert walked to the board and began writing down the hymns the group called out. Our assignment was narrowing the list to twelve, but we couldn't do it. In fact, it was a challenge to keep the list to forty-eight! So the meeting to discuss a single hymn book became a vision to publish four.

The first project, *O Worship the King*, included some of the first hymns we wrote on the board; *O Come, All Ye Faithful* featured some great Christmas hymns; and *What Wondrous Love Is This* highlighted the wonder of Easter.

And with this book, the fourth in the *Great Hymns of Our Faith* series, our adventure of creating these four volumes has concluded with hymns about hope and heaven.

We have had the joy of discovering the deep roots of these hymns—meeting men and women from centuries past who walked with God. We have looked into Holy Scripture and discovered the reason why these hymns have changed the lives of those who have sung them over the years. And we've had the privilege of recording these hymns with the talented students from The Master's College Chorale and their gifted director, Dr. Paul Plew.

And even though we have been singing these hymns since we were children, they have touched us again. Their authors have challenged us, their doctrine has enlightened us, and their melodies have lifted us.

Be this th' eternal song,
Through all the ages on:
May Jesus Christ be praised.

Who can measure the power of a hymn?

Joni Eareckson Tada, Agoura Hills, California
John MacArthur, Sun Valley, California
Robert & Bobbie Wolgemuth, Orlando, Florida

Ernest W. Shurtleff
1862-1917

Henry Smart
1813-1879

Lead on, O King eternal, the day of march has come;
Henceforth in fields of conquest thy tents shall be our home:
Through days of preparation thy grace has made us strong,
And now, O King eternal, we lift our battle song.

Lead on, O King eternal, till sin's fierce war shall cease,
And holiness shall whisper the sweet amen of peace;
For not with swords loud clashing, nor roll of stirring drums,
But deeds of love and mercy, the heav'nly kingdom comes.

Lead on, O King eternal: we follow, not with fears;
For gladness breaks like morning where-e'er thy face appears;
Thy cross is lifted o'er us; we journey in its light:
The crown awaits the conquest; lead on, O God of might.

At the Heart of the Hymn

Joni Eareckson Tada

Since you are my rock and my fortress, for the sake of your name lead and guide me.

—Psalm 31:3

A dreadful silence momentarily seized the banquet hall of the renowned Pearlgate Castle. Over the huge medieval fireplace hung the royal family's coat of arms; and, as if in symbolic defiance, the banner of the Duke of Endor was mounted on the opposite wall. Tension had been building for months between these two powers, and the duke's evil scheme to overthrow Prince Elohim had finally come to a head at this annual feast held for the lords and ladies of the kingdom.

There was a shout and a shoving aside of chairs. Ladies screamed, and dishes clattered to the floor as the strong figure of Prince Elohim leaped to the top of the banquet table. Poised in readiness, he clutched the jewel-encrusted handle of his sword, the weapon given to him by his father, the king. The sleek blade reflected a ray of sunlight, dazzling those who looked on. It was the finest sword in the land. On the floor, surrounding the prince like sharks, paced three of the duke's henchmen, their sabers drawn, awaiting just the right moment to catch Elohim off guard. The prince's eyes flashed from one to the other, watching to see who would strike first. Suddenly steel met steel as two of the soldiers clashed with the prince. He parried their blows, deftly avoiding each jab and thrusting with plunges of his own.

A stab . . . a wound . . . blood! One of the duke's men was down, but in the fray Prince Elohim had been struck. He stole a glance over his shoulder to check his position, but in doing so, his magnificent weapon was knocked from his hand. A gasp escaped from the crowd as ladies drew their kerchiefs to their mouths.

But wait! With deer-like speed, the prince leaped beyond the sweep of his enemies' blades and grabbed a heavy brass candlestick on the table. Armed with a frightfully inferior weapon, he again sprang into the battle, diverting blows with the lamp. He ducked, barely missing a thrust of a knife, but parlayed with a wide swing of the candlestick, breaking the jaw of another opponent. The stunned lone survivor of the duke's force stared in wide-eyed fear. He and Elohim circled one another in silence. The enemy became emboldened at the sight of blood seeping through the prince's sleeve. The prince retreated up the stairs until he was finally pinned against the wall. His puny tool was no match for the razor-sharp sword of his adversary. The enemy lunged, and Elohim jumped aside as the sword sank into a crack between the stones. Before the duke's man could resume his stance, Elohim heaved the massive candlestick into his skull. The final opponent slumped to the floor unconscious.

Drums began rolling, and trumpets sounded. The joyful crowd swarmed around Prince Elohim shouting, "Victory to our prince!" They began to chant a song that became known throughout the land: "With the sword of the king, Prince Elohim is strong; but the candlestick in hand proves him mightier still!" The Duke of Endor was banished forever, and everyone lived happily ever after.

I love adventure stories like this. It's one reason why I love the Bible! It's the fascinating account of how the evil villain, Satan, enslaved the citizens of the kingdom of Earth through treachery and deceit—how he usurped the authority of the rightful Ruler and set up his own rival government. Furthermore, it's the story of how the good Ruler sent His only Son to invade Satan's territory in order to free the captives and retake the kingdom under the family banner. But what is most poignant is that the Son defeated the enemy using "inferior" tactics—servanthood and then death on a cross. It is *this* that proves Him mightier still. For just when the Son was pinned against the wall, just when it seemed He had lost all chance of winning, He overcame in spite of the odds. And the Prince of Peace ends up twice the hero!

And He asks us, His subjects, to follow Him in His battle plan. That's the way

God brings maximum glory to Himself. We are not a jewel-encrusted sword in God's hand. You and I in all of our weakness, in all of our inabilities, are clunky candlesticks doing—by the grace of God—a sword's job. As we persevere and obey, as we put on the armor of God and fight with spiritual weapons, not carnal, we overcome in spite of the odds and end up giving twice the glory to the King. So . . .

Lead on, O King Eternal, till sin's fierce war shall cease,
And holiness shall whisper the sweet amen of peace;
For not with swords loud clashing,
nor roll of stirring drums,
But deeds of love and mercy,
the heav'nly kingdom comes.

In the Light of the Word

John MacArthur

EACH STANZA OF THIS TRIUMPHANT HYMN opens with words borrowed from Paul's benediction in 1 Timothy 1:17: "Now to the King eternal, immortal, invisible, the only God, be honor and glory for ever and ever." It is a marching hymn for the church militant, and it is therefore filled with the language of battle.

The militant theme is fitting, given the New Testament portrayal of the Christian life as warfare. But it is *spiritual* warfare against spiritual forces: "For our struggle is not against flesh and blood, but against the rulers, against the authorities, against the powers of this dark world and against the spiritual forces of evil in the heavenly realms" (Ephesians 6:12).

The Christian life is never characterized in Scripture as a life of ease and comfort (cf. 2 Timothy 2:3). We look forward to eternity, when our dwelling place will be the Father's house—and we know that Christ has already gone there to prepare a place for us (John 14:2-3). When we reach heaven we will rest from our labor (Revelation 14:13). But the present is a time of battle, not rest, and in a figurative sense we are sojourners dwelling in tents on "fields of conquest."

"Days of preparation" for an army are the days spent getting ready for battle. "Preparation day" in Scripture was a technical term that spoke of the day before Sabbath, and especially the day before Passover (cf. Mark 15:42), during which spiritual and practical preparation was made for the observance of a feast-day or a Sabbath-day. The hymn-writer seems to have in mind the spiritual preparation involved in putting on one's spiritual armor (Ephesians 6:13-17). And now it is not a feast or a sabbath rest, but a battle that we enter into.

The hymn makes this crucial confession: "Thy grace has made us strong." Spiritual warfare cannot be fought with fleshly energy. "Woe to those who go down to Egypt for help, who rely on horses, who trust in the multitude of their chariots and in the great strength of their horsemen, but do not look to the Holy One of Israel, or seek help from the LORD" (Isaiah 31:1). The testimony of every true believer is this: "Some trust in chariots and some in horses, but we trust in the name of the LORD our God" (Psalm 20:7). "No king is saved by the size of his army; no warrior escapes by his great strength. A horse is a vain hope for deliverance; despite all its great strength it cannot save. But the eyes of the LORD are on those who fear him, on those whose hope is in his unfailing love" (Psalm 33:16-18).

In Jeremiah 17:5 we read, "This is what the LORD says: 'Cursed is the one who trusts in man, who depends on flesh for his strength and whose heart turns away from the LORD.'" And so in this spiritual warfare we must look to none other for leadership than our "King eternal, immortal, invisible, the only God."

Stanza 2 develops the idea of how spiritual warfare differs from carnal warfare. The goal of victory is not land or power, but divine righteousness. And victory will not be won until "holiness shall whisper the sweet amen of peace."

Moreover, "The weapons we fight with are not the weapons of the world" (2 Corinthians 10:4). It is "not with swords loud clashing," but with "deeds of love and mercy" that we wage war. More specifically, in biblical terms, we fight against Satan's lies with the truth. "We demolish arguments and every pretension that sets itself up against the knowledge of God, and we take captive every thought to make it obedient to Christ" (v. 5).

The closing stanza honors Christ as the one who overcomes our fears by the sheer power of His presence. "We follow, not with fears; for gladness breaks like morning where'er thy face appears." His cross is the standard for our army, and "We journey in its light."

And at the end, "the crown awaits." That is what the apostle Paul looked forward to at the end of his life. He wrote, "I have fought the good fight, I have finished the race, I have kept the faith. Now there is in store for me the crown of righteousness, which the Lord, the righteous Judge, will award to me on that day—and not only to me, but also to all who have longed for his appearing" (2 Timothy 4:7-8).

From Out of the Past

Bobbie Wolgemuth

A YOUNG COLLEGE STUDENT WHO was known among his classmates for his pastime of writing poetry penned the words of this bold hymn. Ernest Shurtleff had graduated from Harvard and was finishing theological studies at Andover Theological Seminary when his fellow students asked him to write something courageous for their commencement exercises. He did not disappoint his friends. In time for the spring commencement ceremony at Andover, twenty-five-year-old Ernest Shurtleff had condensed into three verses this bold call to service and spiritual warfare.

By the time of his graduation from seminary, Ernest had also turned his hobby into two published volumes of poetry. It was a helpful addition to his love of words and poetic imagery that he was also an amateur musician. The ministry that he would have as a minister would be enhanced through his abilities with words and music.

Ernest served as a pastor in California, Massachusetts, and Minnesota as well as having a most productive work in Europe. When he was only thirty-three years old he organized an American church in Frankfurt, Germany.

World War I called on all the resources in the spiritual armory that Ernest had prepared for and written about while in seminary. He and his wife were in their fifties and had already established a ministry to students in Europe when they saw the devastation of the war. Their battle for the souls of the youthful soldiers and students led them to active duty in relief work during the war years.

The triumphant tune that was chosen for the words of "Lead On, O King Eternal" was written by an accomplished organist in Lancashire, England, named Henry Smart. He was a brilliant professional musician and composed this tune, entitled "Lancashire," to be used at a festival in England commemorating the three hundredth anniversary of the Reformation. It is musically full of war and battle tones that lift the Christian singer to bravely hold out against the forces of evil in the world.

Henry was a conductor, composer, and compiler of sacred music and was able to engage his listeners in a spiritual war. He fought his own personal battle with blindness. At fifty-one he found himself totally unable to see, yet continued to compose and play the organ at his church in London until his death at age sixty-six. This brave composer took seriously the words of Psalm 139:12: "Even the darkness is not dark to you; the night is bright as the day, for darkness is as light with you" (ESV).

WILLIAM RALPH FEATHERSTONE
1846-1873

ADONIRAM J. GORDON
1836-1895

My Jesus, I love thee, I know thou art mine;
For thee all the follies of sin I resign.
My gracious Redeemer, my Savior art thou;
If ever I loved thee, my Jesus, 'tis now.

I love thee because thou hast first loved me,
And purchased my pardon on Calvary's tree.
I love thee for wearing the thorns on thy brow;
If ever I loved thee, my Jesus, 'tis now.

I'll love thee in life, I will love thee in death;
And praise thee as long as thou lendest me breath;
And say, when the death-dew lies cold on my brow:
If ever I loved thee, my Jesus, 'tis now.

In mansions of glory and endless delight,
I'll ever adore thee in heaven so bright;
I'll sing with the glittering crown on my brow:
If ever I loved thee, my Jesus, 'tis now.

At the Heart of the Hymn

Joni Eareckson Tada

The LORD your God is with you, he is mighty to save. He will take great delight in you, he will quiet you with his love, he will rejoice over you with singing.

—ZEPHANIAH 3:17

THE MORNING OF MY WEDDING DAY was utterly unique and memorable. And not for reasons you might think. It started in the church bridal salon with my girlfriends laying me down on a couch. They had to shift my paralyzed body this way and that in order to pull my voluminous gown over me. After I was corseted, buttoned, and lifted back into my wheelchair, they gingerly draped my gown over a thin wire mesh covering my wheels so the fabric wouldn't get caught in the spokes. When the organ music began, I wheeled toward the door, stopping for a second in front of a full-length mirror. I looked a little like a float in the Rose Parade.

The glass doors of the sanctuary opened, and I positioned myself at the top of the aisle, breathing deeply to steady my nerves. Just before the wedding march, I glanced down at my gown. I groaned. Somehow I had wheeled over the hem and left a greasy tire mark. My dress hung clumped and uneven—no amount of buckling and binding had helped. My chair was spiffed up, but it was still the big, clunky thing it always was. My bouquet of daisies was off-center on my lap since my paralyzed hands couldn't hold them. I was not the picture-perfect bride you see in magazines.

My last bridesmaid finished her walk down the aisle, and the organ music crescendoed. I inched my chair closer to the last pew, wanting to catch a glimpse of Ken. Suddenly I spotted him way down front, standing at attention and looking tall and elegant in his formal attire. My face grew hot. My heart began to pound. He was craning his neck to look up the aisle. Our eyes met and, amazingly, from that point everything changed.

How I looked no longer mattered. I forgot all about my wheelchair. Grease stains? Flowers out of place? Who cares? No longer did I feel ugly or unworthy; the love in Ken's eyes washed it all away. I was the pure and perfect bride. That's what he saw, and that's what changed me. It took great restraint not to jam my "power stick" into high gear and race down the aisle to reach the front and be with Ken. It was the happiest day of my life.

I think heaven will be a little like that.

At present all we see are our black marks and smudges, and we struggle against sin, feeling far from pure and perfect. We're dismayed that nothing is ever quite *right* with our Christian walk, and we cower and wonder, *Will He ever see anything lovely in me?* It's so frustrating because we are cleansed from our sin, but we're still unclean. We're justified before God, but we've got miles of sanctification to go before we sleep. We're in His household, but we're far from home. Our eyes have been opened, but we can only see through a glass darkly. Most of all, we desire to behold the face of God, and yet we cringe at the prospect.

Maybe this is why it's so hard for us to muster strong feelings about heaven. You and I going to heaven for a wedding? Our wedding to the Lord? What about the dress code? Revelation 19:7-8 says, "'. . . For the wedding of the Lamb has come, and his bride has made herself ready. Fine linen, bright and clean, was given her to wear.' (Fine linen stands for the righteous acts of the saints.)" *Righteous acts?* We glance down at our body of sin and death, thinking everything's tearing apart at the seams.

Getting back to my story, I asked Ken after our wedding if he saw the grease marks. I was wondering if he felt funny seeing his bride sitting in a wheelchair. He shook his head and said, "No, I just thought you were gorgeous. Really."

Wouldn't it be nice if we could believe—really believe—that Jesus would say the same thing? It's a hope we live in. We trust in His love and long and look for Him "while we wait for the blessed hope" (Titus 2:13). And "everyone who has this hope in him purifies himself, just as he is pure" (1 John 3:3). In other words, we fix our eyes on Jesus, believe and obey, all the while trusting He has clothed us in His righteousness. On that glorious Day, all He'll see is our "fine linen, bright and clean." All He'll see is His beautiful bride.

And one look from Him will change us forever. All the stains of earthly life will be purified away just by one searching of those eyes. Our faces will flush, our hearts will pound, for it will be more than we ever dreamed of, more than we ever longed for. And at the sight of our Bridegroom we just might sing . . .

In mansions of glory and endless delight,
I'll ever adore thee in heaven so bright;
I'll sing with the glittering crown on my brow:
If ever I loved thee, my Jesus, 'tis now.

In the Light of the Word

John MacArthur

Few songs in our hymnbook are filled with more emotion than this one. It is a prayer of surrender and faith, poignantly expressing the truest, deepest feeling of every genuine Christian—a powerful, overwhelming love for Christ.

The first line is an expression rich with assurance: "I *know* thou art mine."

That is followed by a declaration of humble repentance: "For thee all the follies of sin I resign." This song was written before anyone ever propounded the notion that it's possible to embrace Jesus as Savior without repenting from sin or surrendering to Christ's lordship. As this song suggests, to receive Christ as Savior with genuine, biblical faith *is* to renounce the follies of sin.

But nonetheless, salvation from sin is accomplished only by divine grace, not by the sinner's own willpower or resolve. And the hymn-writer acknowledges this by referring to Christ as "my gracious Redeemer, my Savior."

Stanza 2 begins with a reference to 1 John 4:19: "We love because he first loved us." At first glance, that may not seem a very noble reason for love: "I love thee because thou hast first loved me." It sounds uncomfortably like the excuse given by the child whose mother asks why he hit his brother: "Because he hit me first!" Reciprocity is never a good motive for how we treat someone else, whether we're talking about retaliating against those who have done us wrong (cf. Romans 12:14) or showing love to people just because they have shown love to us first (cf. Matthew 5:43-44).

But 1 John 4:19 is not talking about the *motive* for our love. It is a humble confession that our hearts are so evil that if God had not sovereignly drawn us to Himself in love, we would never love Him at all. The carnal mind is enmity against God (Romans 8:7-8). If God Himself had not loved us and given us new hearts capable of sincere love for Him, as long as we remained in our fallen state we would have never loved Him on our own. So when we confess that we love because we were first loved by God, we are affirming the sovereignty of God in our salvation.

Christ "purchased my pardon on Calvary's tree" by paying the price of my sins in my place. He wore the "thorns on [His] brow" because He was acting as our substitute, receiving in His own body an infinite measure of the pain and punishment *we* deserve because of our sin. Jesus Himself said, "Greater love has no one than this, that he lay down his life for his friends" (John 15:13). How could we contemplate or sing about such things without echoing the testimony of the chorus: "If ever I loved thee, my Jesus, 'tis now"?

Like so many of the older hymns, this one includes a stanza (stanza 3) that looks ahead to the moment of death—"when the death-dew lies cold on my brow." The songwriter testifies that his love for Christ will endure throughout life and even beyond the grave ("I'll love thee in life, I will love thee in death; and praise thee as long as thou lendest me breath").

In 1 Corinthians 13, the apostle Paul highlights love as the greatest of all virtues, because it endures forever. *Faith* will be swallowed up by sight. *Hope* will eventually be fulfilled. But *love* endures forever. The songwriter is acknowledging the eternality of love in the closing stanza.

And of all earthly loves, it is chiefly *our love for Christ* that will endure throughout eternity—"In mansions of glory and endless delight." The song we'll sing in heaven will be an endless chorus of praise and love for Christ. We will sing of our love for Him "with the glittering crown" on our brows.

There's a poignant irony between stanzas 2 and 4 of this song. In stanza 2, Christ is the one with a crown, and it is an undeserved but painful crown of thorns worn on behalf of sinners. In stanza 4, it is the redeemed sinner who wears a crown, and this is a crown of glory that he also does not deserve, but which was purchased for him with the precious blood of Christ. No wonder we can sing with such deep feeling, "If ever I loved thee, my Jesus, 'tis now."

From Out of the Past

Paul T. Plew

The Canadian poet/hymn-writer William Ralph Featherstone was born on July 23, 1846. Shortly after his conversion to Christianity at the age of sixteen, he penned the words to the awe-inspiring hymn entitled "My Jesus, I Love Thee." Youth today are often creative, talented, idealistic, and highly expectant of others. However, they are often seen as annoying and hard to reach in these "cave years" of life. Imagine a young teenager writing the text to this classic!

The next time you are troubled by the youth in the back row of the church, think of this hymn.

Young William sent the text to his aunt, Mrs. E. Featherstone Wilson. She had it published in *The London Hymn Book* in 1864. However, it appeared anonymously and with a different tune. A song lyric composed by a teenager would certainly be rejected. But the original copy of the author's handwritten poem is not only a part of the family's treasures today, it's proof of William's authorship.

The composer, Adoniram Judson Gordon, named for the pioneer missionary, was born in New Hampshire on April 19, 1836. He was ordained at twenty-seven and six years later became the pastor of the Clarendon Street Baptist Church in Boston. While at this church, he began compiling a hymnal for his congregation. In his search he discovered this anonymous hymn in *The London Hymn Book*. He loved the words but did not think that the text and melody were properly wed. As he meditated on the words one day, "in a moment of inspiration, a beautiful new air sang itself to me."

The hymn in its present form was eventually published in *The Service of Song for Baptist Churches* in 1876, compiled by S. L. Caldwell and A. J. Gordon.

Dr. Gordon never met young William Featherstone, who died at age thirty-six in 1873, three years before Gordon published the hymn.

For well over a century this inspiring devotional hymn has stood beside the great hymns of our Christian heritage. It may be sung in praise and adoration or as a prayer, but always with deep love for a God who loves us so completely.

I'll love thee in life, I will love thee in death;
And praise thee as long as thou lendest me breath.

Uncommon wisdom, maturity, and faith for a sixteen-year-old boy.

RIPPON'S SELECTION OF HYMNS
1787

How firm a foundation, you saints of the Lord,
Is laid for your faith in his excellent Word!
What more can he say than to you he has said,
To you who for refuge to Jesus have fled?

"Fear not, I am with you, O be not dismayed;
For I am your God, and will still give you aid;
I'll strengthen you, help you, and cause you to stand,
Upheld by my righteous, omnipotent hand."

"When through the deep waters I call you to go,
The rivers of sorrow shall not overflow;
For I will be with you, your troubles to bless,
And sanctify to you your deepest distress."

"When through fiery trials your pathway shall lie,
My grace, all-sufficient, shall be your supply;
The flame shall not hurt you; I only design
Your dross to consume and your gold to refine."

"The soul that on Jesus has leaned for repose,
I will not, I will not desert to his foes;
That soul, though all hell should endeavor to shake,
I'll never, no never, no never forsake."

At the Heart of the Hymn

Robert Wolgemuth

My steadfast love I will keep for him forever, and my covenant will stand firm for him.

—Psalm 89:28, ESV

Until then, I hadn't paid that much attention to construction. But right after high school graduation, I took a job with Richard Whitmer & Sons, a small-time contractor in Wheaton, Illinois, where we lived. It was time for me to learn about the building business.

The memory of my first day on the job is still perfectly clear. As I drove up to the site—a new home under construction in Glen Ellyn—a concrete truck was backed up to the edge of a large hole in the ground that had been excavated for the house. I parked my car along the street, walked to the edge, and slid down the embankment. "Grab a shovel," Dick Whitmer shouted over the sound of the truck, already releasing wet concrete down the chute.

Dick moved the chute along what looked like a trench for a narrow sidewalk, filling it with the heavy, gray stuff. I used my shovel to push it and pull it into the forms.

When the truck pulled away, I watched my new boss carefully strike off the concrete inside the wooden framework, leveling it out. With a trowel in his hand, he meticulously smoothed the surface, making certain that everything was "level"—I would soon learn that this was one of his favorite words.

"What is this?" I finally asked, eager to learn what we had just finished.

"This is a footing," he answered.

"What's it for?" I asked.

"The foundation for the house will sit on this," he patiently replied. "If the footings aren't perfectly level [there was that word again], the rest of the house is going to be in serious trouble." He smiled as he spoke.

"Here," he said early one morning a few weeks later, handing me a pickax and a knowing grin. "This is yours." He also gave me a homemade gauge made out of two-by-fours, to be sure that the trench was deep enough—exactly sixteen inches—and wide enough—exactly twenty-four inches—to hold the foundation.

We were about to build a church in Oak Lawn, a small community south of Chicago, and the footings stretched out in an eighty feet by forty feet rectangle. I was going to be introduced to the merciless clay that lies eight feet beneath Illinois coal-black soil. By the end of the day, I had dug 240 feet of trench with my pickax. My hands felt like lead weights dangling at the end of kite string.

Dick checked the forms with his level and the depth of my ditch with his tape measure. He was pleased with my work. I was *very* pleased that he was pleased. Dick Whitmer was meticulous about footings.

Over the next four summers I would learn a lot of things from Dick Whitmer. I learned every trade imaginable. I learned the meaning of great words like *critique* and *accoutrements*. But one of the most important things I learned was how important footings were.

I would also learn that Dick Whitmer was serious about what his life stood on—his own footings. As we'd drive from site to site, he often talked about his love for Jesus and the need for daily obedience to God's Word. He was a diligent student of the Scripture, often quoting favorite passages from the Bible. On Monday mornings I'd often get a detailed summary of his pastor's sermon, filled with the same passion with which it had been delivered the previous day. And he loved world missions. In fact, Dick Whitmer gave so much of his income to the church and to missionaries that his family literally lived from month to month.[1]

From this strong and gentle man, I learned that a man with a sure foundation loves God with all his might and loves his wife and family with unshakable loyalty. And I also learned that the quality of a man's work is a visible demonstration of the condition of his heart. "The Lord will be honored if my work is excellent," he'd tell me.

In July 2001, almost exactly thirty-six years after I had dug my first footer, I got a call from Dick Whitmer's son, Jim. "Dad passed away this afternoon," my friend told me. He also told me that his mother, Dick's wife of more than sixty years, had died only forty-three hours earlier!

The family held a double funeral, celebrating the life and death of their beloved parents.

The First Baptist Church of Wheaton, Illinois, was packed with friends for the funeral service. Visitation had just been held in the Richard Whitmer Fellowship Center. Dick Whitmer left very little behind . . . except for the worldwide influence of his life and the depth of his character. And because of the power of his life, the testimony of his personal sacrifices, and the surety of his witness, Dick Whitmer died a wealthy man.

And his family didn't have to divide any of this between them. All were able to take their portion of his inheritance in full.

The soul that on Jesus has leaned for repose,
I will not, I will not desert to his foes;
That soul, though all hell should endeavor to shake,
I'll never, no never, no never forsake.

Such is the way strong men die.

In the Light of the Word

John MacArthur

This marvelous hymn extols the authority and sufficiency of the Word of God. His Word is indeed a firm foundation for our faith.

Unfortunately, the sufficiency of Scripture is a largely forgotten and unappreciated doctrine in our time. Nowadays the Bible is too often regarded as an archaic and insufficient guide for helping people who struggle with problems such as depression and anxiety. But earlier generations appreciated and clung to the promises of the Bible as the *only* sufficient help for such woes. And this hymn therefore focuses on the scriptural promises that speak to our fears, our depression, and our frustrations.

This is one of the oldest songs in our hymnbook, dating back to a collection of hymns first assembled by John Rippon, who pastored the same London congregation that Charles Spurgeon shepherded a hundred years later.

"What more can he say than to you he has said," the hymn-writer asks, underscoring the perfect sufficiency of God's revealed Word. The writer of Hebrews started his epistle with a similar declaration: "In the past God spoke to our forefathers through the prophets at many times and in various ways, but in these last days he has spoken to us by his Son" (1:1-2). God has spoken, and He has spoken with finality. What He has given us in His Word is everything we need to know for life and godliness. The words of the hymn may actually echo Hebrews 11:32: "And what more shall I say?" Is there more that *needs* to be said? No, or God would have included it in Scripture for us. The truth of Scripture is sufficient "so that the man of God may be thoroughly equipped for every good work" (2 Timothy 3:17).

And for those "who for refuge to Jesus have fled," the promises of Scripture are sufficient to answer every kind of anxiety. They are sufficient to provide help in every kind of sorrow. And they are sufficient to see us through every kind of trial. Each stanza of the hymn recites key promises of Scripture and applies them to the tribulations of our daily lives.

The second stanza is based on the promise of Isaiah 41:10: "Do not fear, for I am with you; do not be dismayed, for I am your God. I will strengthen you and help you; I will uphold you with my righteous right hand." That promise was first given to Isaac in Genesis 26:24: "I am the God of your father Abraham. Do not be afraid, for I am with you." God repeated the same promise to Israel in Deuteronomy 31:6: "Be strong and courageous. Do not be afraid or terrified because of them, for the LORD your God goes with you; he will never leave you nor forsake you." And the promise is reiterated numerous times in Scripture (v. 8; Psalm 27:1-3; 46:1-3; Hebrews 13:5-6).

In other words, the promise of God's enduring presence is the answer to all our fears. "If God is for us, who can be against us?" (Romans 8:31).

Stanzas 3 and 4 are a poetic adaptation of Isaiah 43:1-2: "Fear not, for I have redeemed you; I have summoned you by name; you are mine. When you pass through the waters, I will be with you; and when you pass through the rivers, they will not sweep over you. When you walk through the fire, you will not be burned; the flames will not set you ablaze." God sometimes calls us to go through "rivers of sorrow" and "fiery trials," but always for a good purpose.

In the words of the hymn, "I only design your dross to consume and your gold to refine." That line is a reference to the words of Job in Job 23:10: "He knows the way that I take; when he has tested me, I will come forth as gold."

The final stanza sums up and closes with one more final reference to the familiar promise that is the theme of this hymn and is found in Deuteronomy 31:6, 8; Joshua 1:5; 1 Chronicles 28:20; and Hebrews 13:5: "He will not leave you or forsake you."

From Out of the Past

Bobbie Wolgemuth

THE CHURCH AND CULTURE OF eighteenth-century England was turned upside down by the outspoken beliefs and the hymns of Isaac Watts and John and Charles Wesley. Their influence continued to dominate England in "Dissenting Churches" for over a century. The passion, simplicity, and hymn format practiced by the Reformers provided a blueprint for the coming generations of world changers.

With the same passion of young Watts and the college-age Wesley brothers, the youthful John Rippon set out to inspire the world, waging battle by means of music. He knew Scripture and borrowed its phrases and imagery for both his sermons and his hymns. He selected and edited songs for use in his congregational hymnbook. While editing, he composed the verse, "O that with yonder sacred throng we at His feet may fall; we'll join the everlasting song, and crown him Lord of all" for one of the most powerful hymns of the revival, "All Hail the Power of Jesus' Name."

Rippon compiled a hymnbook in 1787 entitled *A Selection of Hymns from the Best Authors, Intended to Be an Appendix to Dr. Watts' Psalms and Hymns*. It included the first appearance of "How Firm a Foundation," with no author identified except the letter K. Although the lyricist was too humble to affix his name to its publication, the words are a sermon in verse and are commonly attributed to Mr. Keene, who was music director in Dr. Rippon's church. The hymnbook title was shortened simply to *Selection of Hymns*, but its fighting words were poetic verses in the contest for biblical literacy.

Having attended college in Bristol, England, Rippon became pastor of a Baptist church in London at age twenty-four. He served the congregation for over sixty years.

This congregation was familiar with the rough turmoil and dangers brought on by their outspoken beliefs of dissension against the established Anglican policies. Their pastor's hymnal was a weapon stolen directly from Scripture to boost their faith and confidence in an all-sufficient God and His Word. Once the hymns were memorized, the people knew the essential doctrines of the Bible by heart. The valiant weapon was theirs to use all week as they faced hardship.

Rippon's hymnbook gained such popularity that it was published in America and was enthusiastically used by northern and southern states during the Civil War.

More than one tune has been adapted for the words of "How Firm a Foundation." The most widely used is an early American folk melody. Again the composer is unknown, but the music was first noted in Joseph Funk's 1832 collection, *Genuine Church Music*. Five years later it appeared in William Caldwell's *Union Harmony*, identified simply as a southern folk melody. It also was set to John Francis Wade's tune *Adeste Fideles* that accompanies the Christmas hymn "O Come, All Ye Faithful."

"How Firm a Foundation" has touched presidents and military leaders as well as the struggling pilgrims it was originally intended to help. It was a favorite of Teddy Roosevelt and Andrew Jackson, who asked for it to be sung at his bedside before he died in his Tennessee home.

[1] During his lifetime, Richard Whitmer built or remodeled twelve churches. He never took a personal profit from any of these projects. "Whatever you do, work heartily, as for the Lord and not for men, knowing that from the Lord you will receive the inheritance as your reward" (Colossians 3:23-24, ESV).

JOHN NEWTON
1725-1807

Amazing grace!—how sweet the sound—that saved a wretch like me!
I once was lost, but now am found, was blind, but now I see.

'Twas grace that taught my heart to fear, and grace my fears relieved;
How precious did that grace appear the hour I first believed!

Thro' many dangers, toils and snares, I have already come;
'Tis grace has brought me safe thus far, and grace will lead me home.

The Lord has promised good to me, his Word my hope secures;
He will my shield and portion be, as long as life endures.

And when this flesh and heart shall fail, and mortal life shall cease,
I shall possess within the veil a life of joy and peace.

When we've been there ten thousand years, bright shining as the sun,
We've no less days to sing God's praise than when we've first begun.

At the Heart of the Hymn

Joni Eareckson Tada

He replied, "Whether he is a sinner or not, I don't know. One thing I do know. I was blind but now I see!"

—John 9:25

"Was blind, but now I see."

Imagine being blind from birth—never having seen towering thunderheads against an azure sky or a flock of ducks gliding over a glassy lake—and then, in an instant, you are able to see. It'd be nothing short of amazing!

Whenever I sing this line from "Amazing Grace!" I think of the shock of what it would be like to see for the first time. The closest I can come are long-ago Saturday mornings when my neighborhood friends and I would hop the streetcar and head for the Ambassador Theater up at Gywnn Oak Junction. We'd load up on Peanut Chews and stake out seats midway up the aisle, settling in for an afternoon of B-Western movies. Around the time the credits rolled at 3 o'clock, we'd gather our things and head for the lobby. The Ambassador had a pretty small one. As soon as you rounded the corner by the popcorn counter you were blindsided by the dazzle of daylight. There was no vestibule to ease our way from a dark theater into the afternoon sun. The light was such a jolt to our senses, we'd walk outside, rub our eyes, and almost bump into lampposts.

First Peter 2:9 reads a little like a sign posted at the corner of that old lobby, ". . . declare the praises of him who called you *out of darkness into his wonderful light*" (italics mine). As Christians, we've gotten used to having spiritual eyes. We can hardly recall what it was like to be spiritually blind. Yet to be translated from the kingdom of darkness to the kingdom of God's dear Son is nothing short of a blindsiding reality. One second we were in blackness; the next, wonderful daylight. One second we're heading to hell; the next, heaven. We were dead in our sins one moment and alive unto God the next. If we really thought about it, we'd be stumbling, rubbing our eyes, and exclaiming, "What a jolt *this* is!" Amazing!

Sort of like being blind and then suddenly seeing.

Heaven forbid I should ever recover from the shock of being healed from spiritual blindness, the heart-shaking jolt of groping in darkness only to—*wham!*—be hit with light. "Amazing grace!—how sweet the sound that saved a wretch like me" . . . I once was lost and stumbling in the dark . . . "was blind, but now I see."

If you're a Christian and having a little trouble remembering what it was like to live in spiritual darkness and if you want to feel the jolt again, here's an idea . . .

Consider the Gospel as both good news and bad. Want the bad news first? Well, take a breath and swallow this: You are worse—a whole lot worse—than you think. You are more sneaky and devious, more worldly and wicked than the image you project. Pride and peevish thoughts constantly ferment, and a small-minded mean-spiritedness crouches just below the surface of your soul. The bad, *really* bad news is that you are much worse than you believe.

But take heart! God's grace is much greater than you believe. God is a lot—a whole lot—more gracious than you think.[1] And *this* is what makes the good news so great. Love and mercy color His holiness and anger. Forgiveness and patience join His justice and power. Joy and peace kiss His righteousness and wrath. It's a fact. And it's good, *really* good news.

Ponder it for a while. For as you do, you'll begin to feel a rumbling, a jarring way down deep. Meditate a little longer on the good news and—what do you know—you'll get the jolt of your life.

You'll be blindsided with the amazing grace of God. Like stumbling out of darkness and into His wonderful light. And who knows? You might even see things a little more clearly.

IN THE LIGHT OF THE WORD

John MacArthur

THIS MAY BE THE best-known and best-loved hymn in our hymnbooks. It is especially noteworthy for having come from such an unlikely source—the pen of a former slave-trader and brigand who at one time in his life may have seemed the least likely candidate in all the world to write such an enduring hymn.

But this is a hymn about "grace"—the free and unrestrained favor of God that is manifested in the salvation of sinners who have absolutely no merit of their own. Jesus said, "It is not the healthy who need a doctor, but the sick" (Matthew 9:12). Such a glorious tribute to divine grace could only have been written by someone who thought of himself as the chief of sinners (cf. 1 Timothy 1:15).

And yet every genuine Christian ought to be able to sing this hymn earnestly from the heart, because we of all people should understand the utter depravity of our own hearts. There is nothing to commend us to God. Apart from His grace, we are *all* spiritually and morally bankrupt, incapable of loving or obeying God or doing anything to please Him (Romans 8:7-8). Apart from divine grace, there is simply nothing good in us (Romans 7:18).

That's why the apostle Paul wrote, "It is by grace you have been saved, through faith—and this not from yourselves, it is the gift of God—not by works, so that no one can boast" (Ephesians 2:8-9). We simply have nothing to boast about, nothing to be proud of. We are wretched.

At least one denomination has reworded the first line of this hymn in their denominational hymnbook to get rid of the expression "a wretch like me." Some in the denomination apparently felt the expression "wretch" was too demeaning and not healthy for people's sense of self-esteem!

But to be concerned about the sinner's "self-esteem" is to miss the point of grace completely and to nullify the message of this hymn. "God opposes the proud but gives grace to the humble" (James 4:6). Those who are so infatuated with self-esteem that they cannot bring themselves to confess the wretchedness of their own sinful state cannot understand anything of the grace of God. Grace is for the humble, the wretched, the sinner who despairs of rescuing himself from sin.

Jesus' ministry was to the poor, prisoners, the blind, and the oppressed (Luke 4:18). The dregs of society—those who *knew* they were wretched—were the ones upon whom He bestowed grace and compassion. On the other hand, the proud and self-righteous (Pharisees, Sadducees, and rulers of synagogues) met with some of his harshest denunciations. He spent most of His energies with them, showing them what wretches they really were.

The closing phrase of stanza 1 ("was blind, but now I see") echoes the words of the man born blind in John 9. When the angry rulers of the temple demanded that the man denounce Christ as a sinner, he replied, "Whether he is a sinner or not, I don't know. One thing I do know. I was blind but now I see!" (verse 25). The man had no theological training, no ability to articulate an accurate Christology, but one thing he knew: He could see for the first time in his life. That is the universal response of all who have truly been transformed by grace.

The theology of this hymn is as rich and profound as the words are simple. The second stanza says, "'Twas grace that taught my heart to fear." That speaks of the gracious work wrought by the law of God in the hands of the Spirit of God. We are convicted of sin and taught to fear. "The fear of the LORD is the beginning of wisdom" (Psalm 111:10).

The stanza continues: "And grace my fears relieved." That is the gracious work of the Gospel, pointing the sinner to free and full forgiveness, and lifting the burden of sin.

Stanza 4 sings about our ongoing need of grace for daily living. Divine grace is not merely something that intervenes to save us and then leaves us on our own. "He gives us more grace" (James 4:6). God's grace guides us through every step of this life. It has brought us to this point, and it is the guarantee that we will arrive safe in heaven at the end of this life.

The final stanza celebrates the fact that when we do reach heaven at last, we will spend all eternity praising the One who by His grace clothed us in the "bright shining" garments of His own righteousness and transforms us into the likeness of Christ, so that we might spend eternity in praise and fellowship with Him.

From Out of the Past

Bobbie Wolgemuth

ROUGH SEAS AND EVEN rougher sailors surrounded the young Englishman John Newton as he voyaged with his father, the commander of a merchant ship. There were no more Bible stories and soft-spoken devotions from his gentle mother. She had died, and John, at age eleven, was free to roam the Mediterranean with his sea captain father.

John eventually became a ship captain himself, but his merchandise included more than the usual collection of gold, ivory, dyer's wood, and beeswax. His goods were slaves. The despicable practice of capturing strong African boys and jamming them into tiny spaces like common cargo for the long voyage back to England became his lucrative livelihood.

With hours to think and read, Newton taught himself Latin and studied whatever reading material he could lay hold of. It was during this time that he happened upon a copy of Thomas à Kempis's *Imitation of Christ*. The power of this text connected in his soul to his mother's early spiritual tutoring. The seeds of a marvelous conversion to Christianity were sown. Not surprisingly, the intolerable treatment of the captured Africans also began to concern him; then it literally scandalized him. God changed Newton's heart, and the ultimate demise of the slave business in England was set in motion.

John Newton's new life included studying for the ministry while working in

England. Now married, his greatest desire was to preach the Gospel to common folks, young and old. He told the story of his sordid past with candor and gratefulness for God's mercy. His popularity grew, and so did his congregation in Olney, England. A gallery was built in the church to accommodate the growing crowds.

Remembering the powerful influence of his mother's early biblical instruction, he held Thursday afternoon classes for the town children in a large, old manor house. In the same building he began devotional meetings in the evenings for adults.

John used music weekly to instruct the young and old in biblical doctrine and Christian conduct. Not wanting to use the metrical psalms, and unable to find just the right hymnbook that expressed the simple, heartfelt religion he advocated, he began to write hymns himself for the weekly meetings. It was probably when John was in his early forties that the words to "Amazing Grace" were written for one of these prayer meetings. The origin of the tune, although unknown, is an early American folk melody. It may have been one of the songs Newton heard sung by the slaves. Even the melody is a clear demonstration of God's amazing grace.

Newton enlisted his neighbor and articulate poet William Cowper to help with the task of preparing a book of instruction in the Evangelical faith, for singing, reading, and memorizing. The two men met every morning in the beautiful garden between their homes, calling on God for "continual fresh supplies of strength and grace from the fountainhead." God answered their prayer, and the result was the famous book entitled *Olney Hymns*. In addition to "Amazing Grace," Newton's 280 contributions included "How Sweet the Name of Jesus Sounds" and "Glorious Things of Thee Are Spoken." The collection spread all over the English-speaking world.

Newton was in his fifties when he moved to London and grew a large church there. Among those he influenced in the congregation was William Wilberforce, who held a prominent seat in Parliament and was a close friend and adviser to the English Prime Minister. Newton persuaded Wilberforce to use his political life for the service of God. With fearless resolve, Wilberforce took his pastor's advice to heart and campaigned for moral reform and the abolition of the slave trade. In 1833 the House of Commons passed a law emancipating the slaves in all British domains. The influence crossed the ocean, and later America also set all her slaves free.

Blind at the time of his death, at age eighty-two, John Newton said, "My memory is nearly gone, but I remember two things, that I am a great sinner, and that Christ is a great Savior."

[1] This illustration is not original with me, but with Dr. Jack Miller, formerly of Westminster Theological Seminary.

German 1800
Translated by Edward Caswall
1814-1878

Sir Joseph Barnby
1838-1896

When morning gilds the skies, my heart awaking cries:
May Jesus Christ be praised.
Alike at work and prayer to Jesus I repair:
May Jesus Christ be praised.

When sleep her balm denies, my silent spirit sighs:
May Jesus Christ be praised.
When evil thoughts molest, with this I shield my breast:
May Jesus Christ be praised.

Does sadness fill my mind? A solace here I find:
May Jesus Christ be praised.
Or fades my earthly bliss? My comfort still is this:
May Jesus Christ be praised.

In heav'n's eternal bliss the loveliest strain is this:
May Jesus Christ be praised.
The pow'rs of darkness fear, when this sweet chant they hear:
May Jesus Christ be praised.

Let earth's wide circle round in joyful notes resound:
May Jesus Christ be praised.
Let air and sea and sky, from depth to height, reply:
May Jesus Christ be praised.

Be this, while life is mine, my canticle divine:
May Jesus Christ be praised.
Be this th' eternal song, through all the ages on:
May Jesus Christ be praised.

At the Heart of the Hymn

Robert Wolgemuth

I want to be the kind of person whose first waking thought is "Good morning, Lord," not, "Good Lord, morning."

—Robert A. Cook

It happens in the early morning darkness of major cities all over the world. They call it "rush hour," but for most of the folks sitting perfectly still in miles-long parking lots, this phenomenon is unfittingly named. Rush hour? I don't think so.

Helicopters above stream up and down these steel-and-glass-lined concrete corridors transmitting the bad news over the radio.

"I'm over the Santa Ana near Chapman. It's a mess down there."

"Avoid the LBJ. There's a multiple-car wreck just east of Prestonwood."

"It's going to take you forty minutes from Hillside to the Loop. The Eisenhower is backed up all the way from Mannheim to Cicero."

"Problem in the Lincoln Tunnel. Traffic is backed up all the way to the eastern spur of the turnpike. If you head for the Holland, it's not much better."

Helicopter propeller blades emit a palpable *woop woop woop woop* sound. These sky jockeys give themselves clever names like Traffic Jam Jim and U-Turn LaVerne, but no one's smiling. And though the news they're transmitting is interesting, for those folks sitting in their cars below, it's *not* news.

The sun peeks over the eastern sky, tossing beams of light between skyscrapers and billboards onto the motorcade. The glow casts an iridescent outline on the underside of the clouds above. Colors burst from the grayness: rose, orange, magenta. It's a breathtaking spectacle—one that would melt the heart of the most crusted cynic. But no one notices. No one sees anything at all.

Men keep clacking away on their cell phones. Women tilt their rearview mirrors to double-check their hair and makeup in the sunlight.

No one looks up.

In 1988, during the years that my friend Mike Hyatt and I owned a publishing company, we received many unsolicited manuscripts. I remember the premise of one of these. Although we chose not to publish the book, the writer was suggesting that we should take the opportunity to lift our hearts and pray during unpredicted down times, in-limbo times, time-killing times—like waking up in the middle of the night or waiting in a doctor's office . . . or sitting in traffic.[1]

Of course, I knew that prayer was important in my scheduled quiet times, before meals, with the family, and in Bible studies and church. But I had never considered that God may be putting me in these helpless situations to draw me into His courts.

So I tried it. In the midnight darkness of my bedroom, or sitting in a chair-lined room faced with two-year-old copies of *Popular Mechanics* magazines, or in the dawdling procession of four-wheeled caterpillars . . . I'd look up. I'd pray.

And in His kindness the Lord filled the space with names of people to pray for.

"Lord, please bless Sam. Maybe he's facing some stiff pressure today at the office. I pray that you'll give him Your creativity, Your peace, Your wisdom."

I'd shoot off a quick e-mail to Sam the next day and amazingly, he *was* in the middle of an unusually challenging time in his business. In His providence and perfect timing, the Lord had given me the privilege of bringing a good friend to the throne of grace.

Like the sunlight gilding the underside of a morning cloud and granting it a magnificent radiance, God had taken some of the unspeakably frustrating moments in my life and turned them into a sanctuary.

No longer would I complain (as much) about these uncontrolled situations of time loss and frustration. Now they were gifts to give me special entry into the presence of my heavenly Father.

Alike at work and prayer
To Jesus I repair [eagerly go].
May Jesus Christ be praised.

IN THE LIGHT OF THE WORD

John MacArthur

IT IS HARD TO THINK OF A MORE fitting hymn of pure praise for Christ than this one. Its title is reminiscent of Psalm 108:2-3: "I will awaken the dawn. I will praise you, O Lord, among the nations; I will sing of you among the peoples."

True praise begins early, "when morning gilds the skies" (cf. Psalm 5:3; 63:1; 130:6). But praise is also appropriate for any time of the day and in the midst of any activity, "alike at work or prayer." The psalmist wrote, "Evening, morning and noon I cry out" (Psalm 55:17). The apostle Paul wrote, "pray continually; give thanks in all circumstances, for this is God's will for you in Christ Jesus" (1 Thessalonians 5:17-18). "Pray in the Spirit on all occasions with all kinds of prayers and requests" (Ephesians 6:18). Praise should fill all our prayers, and we should pray without ceasing.

The refrain of this hymn, repeated twice in each stanza (once at the end of each couplet), is simple and straightforward: "May Jesus Christ be praised." Nothing is more moving than hearing this hymn sung by a large congregation. It never fails to remind me of Philippians 2:9-11: "Therefore God exalted [Christ] to the highest place and gave him the name that is above every name, that at the name of Jesus every knee should bow, in heaven and on earth and under the earth, and every tongue confess that Jesus Christ is Lord, to the glory of God the Father."

This hymn speaks of the power of praise to lift our hearts above the darkness of our trials and the woes of this earthly life. Scripture says, "Resist the devil, and he will flee from you" (James 4:7). One effective way to resist Satan when he accuses or discourages us is to fix our hearts on Christ and praise Him.

The closing stanza reminds us that praise to Christ ought to be the constant theme of all our songs throughout life and eternity. "Be this, while life is mine, my canticle divine . . ." and "Be this th' eternal song, through all the ages long: May Jesus Christ be praised."

That perspective is what draws me again and again to the classic hymns of the faith. We will spend eternity praising Christ in song. The apostle Paul said this is the very purpose for which God redeemed us. In fact, in a positional sense, He has already "raised us up with Christ and seated us with him in the heavenly realms in Christ Jesus, in order that in the coming ages he might show the incomparable riches of his grace, expressed in his kindness to us in Christ Jesus" (Ephesians 2:6-7).

In the apostle John's descriptions of his heavenly vision, again and again he describes the praise that takes place constantly in heaven: "Day and night they never stop saying: 'Holy, holy, holy is the Lord God Almighty, who was, and is, and is to come'" (Revelation 4:8).

And Christ is the object of heaven's praise, too. Revelation 5:11-14 describes the praise that takes place before His heavenly throne:

> *Then I looked and heard the voice of many angels, numbering thousands upon thousands, and ten thousand times ten thousand. They encircled the throne and the living creatures and the elders. In a loud voice they sang: "Worthy is the Lamb, who was slain, to receive power and wealth and wisdom and strength and honor and glory and praise!" Then I heard every creature in heaven and on earth and under the earth and on the sea, and all that is in them, singing: "To him who sits on the throne and to the Lamb be praise and honor and glory and power, for ever and ever!" The four living creatures said, "Amen," and the elders fell down and worshiped.*

So no earthly activity is more heavenly than singing Christ's praise here and now, without ceasing. This hymn is a wonderful reminder of the simplicity—and yet the profundity—of our praise. The substance of our praise is straightforward and to the point. And yet no matter how many times we repeat it, it is a message brimming with eternal significance: "May Jesus Christ be praised."

FROM OUT OF THE PAST

Bobbie Wolgemuth

SEARCHING FOR BEAUTIFUL AND exquisite poetry in Latin and German was like a treasure hunt for the gifted Edward Caswall. He was a man of culture and scholarship, speaking and writing in several languages. When he found a song in a German hymnbook dated 1828, without the author's name, he was drawn to its poetic grace and tender beauty. His poetic sensitivity and artistic genius fashioned six of the fourteen stanzas from the anonymous poem into the English hymn "When Morning Gilds the Skies." The depth and tenderness of his nature was immediately evident, and the song became a favorite of English-singing congregations.

The times in England in the 1830s were chaotic due to the Industrial Revolution. Industry had moved from home and villages to large factories with the introduction of the steam engine. Because machines could cultivate multiple acres, farmers laid off hired hands. Power looms were putting small weavers out of business. With no child labor laws, children were working long hours to make cloth in factories. The result was human tragedy and despair. Upheaval and riots began. Rebellious people connected their misery in part with the failure of the established church to cope with their real needs. They needed jobs. They saw the clergy as privileged, selfish, and uncaring of the social and political condition of the displaced and despairing people.

It was against this backdrop that upon graduation from college in Oxford, England, Edward became an Anglican clergyman. Later he converted into the Catholic Church and continued to be a servant-leader. He cared for the people, responded with sensitivity to the unfortunate, and wrote verses that showed the depth and tenderness of his nature. In addition to all his self-effacing service, Edward was devoted to the study of ancient ecclesiastical history, doctrine, liturgy, and hymnody.

After the death of his wife when he was in his early thirties, Edward spent much time at the country retreat of his mentor and the leader of the Oxford Movement, John Henry Newman. It was a fascinating place for a scholar like Edward, for it had an extensive library with over ten thousand volumes, mostly on the history of the church. The retreat provided rest and refreshment on a nine-acre farm with a sloping hillside and the shelter of old trees. It was a perfect place for Edward to read, study, write, and translate the rare treasures he found in the library.

With a passion to restore truth to church liturgy, Caswall brought new fervor and reverence into public worship through the quality of his verse. He used his gifts to raise the standard of church music and enrich the liturgy. Many scholars tried their hand at the work of translating, but few were as successful as Edward. His translation of "Jesus, the Very Thought of Thee" from a Latin hymn is among the most beloved and widely used.

Sir Joseph Barnby composed the tune for this hymn of praise. As a boy, Joseph sang in a prestigious boys choir in York, England. He chose music as his field of study and became a leading composer and one of England's most distinguished choral conductors. When he was fifty-four years old, Queen Victoria knighted Barnby in honor of his excellent work and achievements in music. In this hymn, his outstanding melody carries Caswall's verses with an upward lilt and a bright pace that expresses the joy of morning praise lifted like the freshness of a glorious sunrise.

The translation of the first four stanzas of "When Morning Guilds the Skies" became so popular in England that Caswall kept translating more of the Latin. By the time he was sixty, he had rendered all fourteen verses of the original German into English. When he died at age sixty-four, he was buried on the beautiful hillside in the tiny retreat cemetery near the beloved comrades who had studied ancient manuscripts and labored in love with him.

[1] If I remembered the unpublished author's name, I'd give her the credit she deserves for this wonderful idea right here.

WILLIAM WILLIAMS
1717-1781

JOHN HUGHES
1873-1932

Guide me, O thou great Jehovah, pilgrim through this barren land;
I am weak, but thou art mighty; hold me with thy pow'rful hand;
Bread of heaven, Bread of heaven, feed me till I want no more,
Feed me till I want no more.

Open now the crystal fountain, whence the healing stream doth flow;
Let the fire and cloudy pillar lead me all my journey through;
Strong Deliv'rer, strong Deliv'rer, be thou still my strength and shield,
Be thou still my strength and shield.

When I tread the verge of Jordan, bid my anxious fears subside;
Death of death, and hell's Destruction, land me safe on Canaan's side;
Songs of praises, songs of praises I will ever give to thee,
I will ever give to thee.

At the Heart of the Hymn

Robert Wolgemuth

Lead me in the path of your commandments, for I delight in it.

—Psalm 119:35, ESV

Dean Kamen barely graduated from high school, but the shy youngster's problem wasn't ignorance. Actually, he loved to learn. It's just that he was intimidated because he thought that he was the only person in his class who wasn't getting it. So he sat quietly.

Then one day in physics class, Dean read a short account of the life of Sir Isaac Newton in his textbook. But he wasn't satisfied. He wanted to know more about the man some consider to be the greatest scientist who ever lived. So Dean Kamen went to the library and, instead of checking out books *about* Newton, found a copy of Newton's own work, *Principia*.

The teenager pored over the book. "All matter attracts all other matter with a force proportional to the product of their masses and inversely proportional to the square of the distance between them." The teenager's heart raced.

"Be courageous and steady to the Laws," Newton wrote, "and you cannot fail." Dean Kamen was swept away not only with Newton's brilliance but with the overwhelming anticipation of what his own study of science would bring to him.

Kamen enrolled in college but flunked out. "I never went to class anyway," he confessed. "There were more interesting things happening in my parents' basement."

With an indomitable spirit to learn and create, Dean Kamen became an inventor. His first discovery—an automatic syringe—was completed by the time he was twenty-five years old. With the sale of this invention, Dean became a millionaire and never looked back.

Today Dean Kamen holds over 150 patents, including innovations in medical technology and robotic sciences. But perhaps his most important invention is the Segway, a two-wheeled electric scooter that Kamen says will be "to the car what the car was to the horse and buggy." For ten years Dean Kamen—along with 200 engineers—spent over $100 million to perfect the Segway.

The magic of this scooter is its "brain" containing two electronic controller circuit boards, two batteries, and a cluster of microprocessors. And because the Segway also contains five gyroscopes[1] it cannot fall down—it can't even be forced to fall over. The stabilizing system in this little forty-five-pound machine rivals the technology found in the cockpit of a jumbo jet. When you step onto the Segway and begin to move, you will not fall down. Imagine having that kind of confidence in a safe journey.

What could be better than this . . . unless, of course, your guidance system is the living God, the Creator of the universe?

I will instruct you and teach you in the way you should go;
I will counsel you with my eye upon you.
—Psalm 32:8, ESV

On my forty-fourth birthday I received the phone call every entrepreneur dreads. "I'm calling your note," the banker on the other end said. "This isn't my choice," he added. "But I'm a man under authority, and I have to do what I have to do."

In a few minutes I was meeting with my business partner to tell him the news. Then we met with our employees, informing them that our company would be closing its doors. In that instant my net worth went to zero.

For years I had said that I trusted God. As a layman I had taught many Sunday school lessons on His goodness and His sovereignty. But for the first time in my life I was faced with a black hole of my own . . . an uncertain future. What was I to do?

I picked up the phone and called Bobbie. When I heard her voice, I broke down and cried like a little boy. "It's over," were the only words I could speak. She told me that she loved me. "We'll get through this together," she added.

As I pulled my car into the driveway that evening, my mind raced. I had leveraged everything on this business. Now we would have to sell the house and tell our college daughter that we could no longer afford her tuition payments.

Bobbie greeted me at the door. Lots of tears were shed. We walked into the living room and sat down on the sofa. I told her the details of what had happened and what this would mean to our family. We held each other's hands and prayed.

Bobbie and I took a deep breath and stepped onto our "spiritual Segways." An unexpected calm came over us. We were not afraid.

I am weak, but thou art mighty;
Hold me with thy pow'rful hand.

In the Light of the Word

John MacArthur

The psalmist in Psalm 48:14 wrote, "This God is our God for ever and ever; he will be our guide even to the end." William Williams develops the idea of God as our guide in this classic expression of the sinner's utter dependence on the all-wise leadership of a loving and attentive God.

The hymn is filled with imagery from the journeys of the Israelites in the wilderness of Sinai under Moses. The "barren land" the hymn-writer has in mind is this earthly life, of course. Like Sinai, its terrain is hostile to the journey. The climate is not conducive to comfort. Provisions are scarce. But with God to guide us we have nothing to fear.

The hymn further reminds us that while we are "weak," God is "mighty," and He sustains us with His omnipotent hand. Similar expressions are used often in

Scripture. In Psalm 18:35, for example, David writes, "Your right hand sustains me." The context pictures God sovereignly assisting a warrior in battle, steadying him so that he does not fall.

The psalmist in Psalm 73 uses the same imagery in a similar, but even more personal, way. In verse 23 he addresses God: "I am always with you; you hold me by my right hand." That seems to picture God as a tender and loving Father, clinging to the believer's hand to give support, comfort, encouragement, and strength.

God Himself speaks these words of fatherly kindness to the Israelites in Isaiah 41:13: "I am the LORD, your God, who takes hold of your right hand and says to you, Do not fear; I will help you." So when the hymn-writer says, "Hold me with thy pow'rful hand," he is using a childlike expression of trust and reliance.

The closing thought of the first stanza is a recognition of the believer's absolute dependence on God for sustenance, and a bold plea that God's gracious provision will be abundant enough to fill every last longing ("feed me till I want no more.")

The "Bread of heaven" for the Israelites in the wilderness was manna, of course. But manna itself was a symbol of Christ. Like Him, it came down from heaven and was offered freely and sufficiently. It should have satisfied the Israelites completely. Nonetheless, they *weren't* satisfied, and they demanded something more (Numbers 11:4-6).

But the manna also had a spiritual lesson, as Moses reminded the Israelites after their wilderness wanderings were over: "He humbled you, causing you to hunger and then feeding you with manna, which neither you nor your fathers had known, to teach you that man does not live on bread alone but on every word that comes from the mouth of the LORD" (Deuteronomy 8:3).

Jesus said the manna in Moses' time was not the *true* "Bread of heaven." It was only a symbol of a greater reality. He said, "I tell you the truth, it is not Moses who has given you the bread from heaven, but it is my Father who gives you the true bread from heaven. For the bread of God is he who comes down from heaven and gives life to the world. . . . I am the bread of life. He who comes to me will never go hungry, and he who believes in me will never be thirsty" (John 6:32-35).

Stanza 2 invokes still more imagery from the Israelites' wilderness wanderings. The "crystal fountain" is a reference to the water that came from a rock in the wilderness (Exodus 17:6; Numbers 20:8-11). That, too, symbolized Christ as the source of all our refreshment (1 Corinthians 10:4). The "fire" and "cloudy pillar" were the visible manifestations of divine glory that led the Israelites throughout their wilderness journeys (Exodus 13:21-22).

The closing line of stanza 2 is a reference to Psalm 140:7: "O Sovereign LORD, my strong deliverer, who shields my head in the day of battle." It also borrows from the words of Psalm 28:7: "The LORD is my strength and my shield."

The final stanza pictures the end of life's journey like the end of the Israelites' wanderings—at the "verge of Jordan," prepared to enter the Promised Land, eager to be "safe on Canaan's side," where forever we will sing "songs of praises" to the One who has led us and delivered us.

FROM OUT OF THE PAST

Bobbie Wolgemuth

BORN IN WALES IN A stone farmhouse with a huge stone hearth and fireplace, William Williams would grow up to ignite the stone-cold hearts of Wales with the fire of his hymns. As a boy, he worked on the farm and prepared to take medical courses and become a doctor. Perhaps his interest in medicine was intensified because of the six children born to his parents; he alone survived to adulthood. His plans for medical school were drastically altered, however, when he met an enthusiastic young Welsh revivalist named Howell Harris.

William was twenty years old and curious to hear the man who was preaching to enormous crowds and causing great spiritual upheaval in the country. William encountered a passionate twenty-four-year-old preaching in a churchyard one Sunday morning to parishioners as they left their regular service. The spirited message of Howell Harris captured young William's heart, and he immediately changed his course of study from medicine of the body to medicine for the soul.

William's gift of music and poetic verse was quickly enlisted as the ordained vehicle to spread the Gospel throughout Wales. Until that time, there were no songs to carry the message of biblical truth to the Welsh people. They, however, were great singers. Their bards had sung the deeds of warriors and national heroes from earliest times. The new converts made up a hearty congregation of singers—the unchurched, the socially outcast, the poor, the ignorant, and the criminal mingled with the comfortable and the educated.

William rejected the notion of the day that emotion and affections need not be involved in salvation or church music. Allowing for feeling and in no way despising warm waves of emotion while hearing the Word of God, he continued to raise the standard by writing hymns that roused the singer from lethargy to life. He wrote eight hundred hymns, all in Welsh. And like all Welshmen, his love of nature's elegance was intertwined with his religion.

He loved the beauty of his land's native rolling hills, grand mountains, and the sea breaking on rocky shores. His poetic imagery interwoven with biblical imagery endeared him to every heart.

Hymns could be learned quickly and had inspirational power second only to preaching. Those who could not read caught on by ear; others learned to read so they could enjoy hymns in public or private worship. Ensuring the triumph of the revival, the new music was also becoming a fierce educational and cultural force.

With all of Wales as his parish, William traveled by horse or on foot thousands of miles. The words of the Bible became his familiar and most loved companion as he trudged through the snow, walked in the rain, and endured the heat of the sun and the attacks by crowds of ruffians who tried to stop his preaching. The chief source of his influence on the country continued to be the great hymns he wrote.

Drawing all his imagery from the Bible he knew so well, William penned

"Guide Me, O Thou Great Jehovah" when he was twenty-eight. It remained only in the Welsh language until he was in his fifties, when it came into the English language and found its way around the world.

John Hughes composed the tune for the hymn for a Welsh song festival in 1905. The rousing melody is a favorite with congregations far beyond the borders of Wales. His wife recalled that he wrote it one Sunday morning in the chapel of the Baptist church where he served as pastor. This hymn's certain popularity was greatly boosted by its frequent use in the trenches of Flanders in the First World War. It was sung so lustily by the Welsh soldiers that German troops began to sing it as well. The words that had sustained the young preacher who walked the hills of Wales could fortify the young soldiers' spirits like nothing else. There is no boundary to music that strengthens the heart of young men.

[1] A gyroscope is a spinning wheel inside a stable frame. The spinning object stays on course because it resists changes to its axis of rotation.

CHARLES WESLEY
1707-1788

JOHN ZUNDEL
1815-1882

Love divine, all loves excelling, Joy of heav'n, to earth come down:
Fix in us thy humble dwelling, all thy faithful mercies crown:
Jesus, thou art all compassion, pure, unbounded love thou art;
Visit us with thy salvation, enter ev'ry trembling heart.

Breathe, O breathe thy loving Spirit into ev'ry troubled breast;
Let us all in thee inherit, let us find the promised rest:
Take away the love of sinning; Alpha and Omega be;
End of faith, as its Beginning, set our hearts at liberty.

Come, Almighty to deliver, let us all thy life receive;
Suddenly return, and never, nevermore thy temples leave.
Thee we would be always blessing, serve thee as thy hosts above,
Pray, and praise thee, without ceasing, glory in thy perfect love.

Finish, then, thy new creation; pure and spotless let us be:
Let us see thy great salvation perfectly restored in thee;
Changed from glory into glory, till in heav'n we take our place,
Till we cast our crowns before thee, lost in wonder, love, and praise.

At the Heart of the Hymn

Joni Eareckson Tada

For I am convinced that neither death nor life, neither angels nor demons, neither the present nor the future, nor any powers, neither height nor depth, nor anything else in all creation, will be able to separate us from the love of God that is in Christ Jesus our Lord.

—Romans 8:38-39

As I sang these hymns about heaven on the accompanying CD, something splendid was happening in my heart. I found myself longing and looking forward to heaven in a fresh, new way. And it was ecstatic.

When I sang "Love Divine, All Loves Excelling," I found the Lord lifting me into the stratosphere of celestial air, pumping my heart and pressing my thoughts up against the pearly gates. The hymn left me breathless. Soon heaven will arrive, and we will be in the embrace of our Savior. We will no longer look through a glass darkly but will see the whole universe in plain sight. We will burn with the brilliant newness of being clothed in righteousness, and joy will enthrall and enrapture, swirling us up to the heights of heaven in a rushing torrent of praise.

You and I will then race to the crest of a hill where we shall see great multitudes of people happily running through meadows of lilies, rushing down banks of violets, all of them pulsing with light, flying with birds, and laughing with angels. Someone will shout, "Are we all here?" and another will say, "Yes, we're all here!" All believers will be there.

Then suddenly in crystal-clear glory, the holy city, the New Jerusalem, will descend from the highest heaven, sparkling like a prism. All gates everywhere will open, and with trumpets resounding we shall walk as sons and daughters of

God into the grand banquet hall with a thousand banners from every nation waving above us. The hall will be alive in light so bright you can smell it, joy so thick you can touch it, and music so happy you can breathe it. Together we will take our seats at the wedding supper of the Lamb ". . . like a great multitude, like the roar of rushing waters and like loud peals of thunder, shouting: 'Hallelujah! For our Lord God Almighty reigns. Let us rejoice and be glad and give him glory! For the wedding of the Lamb has come, and his bride has made herself ready'" (Revelation 19:6-7).

Our Bridegroom, our Husband and Father, God and Savior, Jesus Christ Himself, shall fill the room. Somehow, some way He will look into your eyes and mine and melt away every sad thought about Earth. Its disappointments will be but a dim dream—only happy thoughts will survive, and, in fact, their joy will find the complete heavenly fulfillment that Earth only hinted of. We, the body of Christ, will enjoy our fulfillment, too—we will be completely *one* as Christ always intended us to be. That fact alone will multiply our joy exponentially as we look up and down the banquet table.

There will be Moses toasting Martin Luther, St. Augustine giving a jungle missionary a big bear hug. Fanny Crosby will be humming a tune with the widow who faithfully played the rickety piano at the nursing home every Sunday. And St. Paul will be leaning on his elbow, asking you about your testimony.

Then the great banquet hall will become quiet. For Jesus shall do a most amazing thing. He will serve us in the style of Isaiah 25:6: "On this mountain the LORD Almighty will prepare a feast of rich food for all peoples, a banquet of aged wine—the best of meats and the finest of wines."

Our lovely Savior will lift a cup of the finest of those fine wines. It will be the very cup about which He spoke in Matthew 26:29: "I tell you, I will not drink of this fruit of the vine from now on until that day when I drink it anew with you in my Father's kingdom." We then shall drink of Him to our hearts content and be utterly and completely home, safe, happy, and at rest.

What a vision! Will it be anything like I have described in heaven? Only God knows. But I can still dream, and I can sing with celestial air the last verse of "Love Divine, All Loves Excelling":

Finish, then, thy new creation; pure and spotless let us be:
Let us see thy great salvation perfectly restored in thee;
Changed from glory into glory, till in heav'n we take our place,
Till we cast our crowns before thee, lost in wonder, love, and praise.

In the Light of the Word

John MacArthur

One of the best-loved and most enduring of Charles Wesley's voluminous hymns is this poetic prayer that the love of Christ will be perfected in us. Christ is personified in the first stanza as "Love divine . . . Joy of heav'n, to earth come down." He Himself is "all compassion, pure, unbounded love." So this hymn is not a prayer about an emotion or sentiment called love; it is an invitation for Christ to indwell us as the very embodiment of God's love.

The apostle Paul wrote that love is the greatest of all virtues (1 Corinthians 13:13). The hymn-writer echoes that when he speaks of love as the crown of all mercies.

So the first stanza honors Christ. In the second stanza, the Holy Spirit is the theme. The stanza begins with a reference to John 20:22, when Jesus breathed on His disciples and said, "Receive the Holy Spirit." Of course, all believers are permanently indwelt by the Holy Spirit. Under the New Covenant, God promises, "I will put my Spirit in you" (Ezekiel 36:27). Every true believer is a temple of the Holy Spirit (1 Corinthians 6:19). So when the hymn pleads for the impartation of the Holy Spirit, this must not be interpreted as a plea for something that occurs subsequent to saving faith. Nor should we imagine that we must pray for the Holy Spirit to be imparted afresh, repeatedly, into our hearts as Christians. The hymn merely expresses the believer's concurrence and consent in accordance with Luke 11:13 ("How much more will your Father in heaven give the Holy Spirit to those who ask him!").

Wesley's original words in this stanza were unfortunately tainted with perfectionist theology and second-blessing terminology learned from his famous brother. (He spoke of finding a "second rest" and prayed that God would "take away our bent to sinning.") But modern editors have adapted the words to make them more biblical. The stanza is a prayer for spiritual rest and a pure heart, reminiscent of many passages in the Psalms (e.g., 51:10; 132:14).

The final line of stanza 2 ("End of faith, as its beginning") is probably an oblique reference to Paul's rebuke in Galatians 3:3: "Are you so foolish? After beginning with the Spirit, are you now trying to attain your goal by human effort?" Entrance into the Christian life is by faith; and faith, not human effort, is the means to our end. "So then, just as you received Christ Jesus as Lord, continue to live in him" (Colossians 2:6).

As the first stanza focuses on Christ and the second on the Holy Spirit, the third stanza seems to have the First Person of the Trinity in view: "Come, Almighty to deliver." That echoes the language of Isaiah 63:1, where God is described as "mighty to save."

The phrase "suddenly return, and never, nevermore thy temples leave" is only slightly problematic theologically. We know, of course, that God does not depart once He indwells a believer. "Never will I leave you; never will I forsake you" (Hebrews 13:5). Yet from the believer's perspective, it sometimes seems as if our sin has caused God to be so grieved with us that His presence has deserted us. Thus David prayed in Psalm 51:11, "Do not cast me from your presence or take your Holy Spirit from me." The plea of this hymn is similar; it is the natural expression of a repentant heart.

The remainder of stanza 3 expresses the desire of the believer's heart to serve

God perfectly and without interruption, as the angels ("hosts above") do. So the hymn-writer looks forward eagerly to heaven, when we will be able to "pray, and praise . . . without ceasing."

The apostle Paul says you can be confident "that he who began a good work in you will carry it on to completion until the day of Christ Jesus" (Philippians 1:6). The final stanza of the hymn anticipates that perfection in eternal glory, when we will finally be "pure and spotless."

The phrase "changed from glory into glory" is a quotation from 2 Corinthians 3:18, which describes the process by which we are conformed to the image of Christ, "transformed into his likeness with ever-increasing glory." And finally, in heaven, we will honor God by laying our crowns before his throne (Revelation 4:10), "lost in wonder, love, and praise."

From Out of the Past

Bobbie Wolgemuth

It was in the social and religious chaos of eighteenth-century England that Charles Wesley was destined to help start a revolution with the hymns he penned. And because his pen was dipped in the irresistible love of the Savior, the whole of society was changed: morality, health, politics, prisons, class barriers, slavery, education, literature, music, and religion.

Charles and his older brother John were brokenhearted over the deplorable class struggle in England. Social and religious cultures were dangerously intertwined, degrading peasants and the working class poor with greed, bribes, and taxation.

The Anglican Church was a strong defender of the monarchy, and privileged wealth flowed freely between the two. Bishop appointments and churches were "for sale." Some drew tax revenues of $100,000 a year and in exchange were indebted to the monarchy. Privileged rectors would hire "curates" to look after each parish, paying him a pittance and pocketing the rest of the income. The true shepherd of the people could hardly feed his family with the tiny allotment.

One of the poor working parsons who was mistreated and underpaid was Samuel Wesley, John and Charles's father. The boys grew up seeing the injustice of the system and the contrasting love and care their parents lavished upon their parishioners. These two young boys were tutored from earliest youth to stand against this blasphemy. The legacy of faith and love demonstrated by Samuel and Susanna Wesley was the blueprint for the Methodist Movement that would change all of Europe, lead to the abolition of slavery, and remake the social structure of the world.

From their knees, Charles and his brother John changed the world. They had prayed from earliest childhood. They sang prayers before breakfast as little boys. They prayed for the enemies who burned their church down. They thanked God for the good friends from the church who climbed on each other's shoulders to lower John from the burning rectory and save him from the fire. They prayed for their father who had been put in jail for dissenting. They prayed for the people who came to their home for Sunday services. They sat on the floor in their cottage when people came for weekly prayer meetings. They heard their mother pray for them and with them every day as she homeschooled all of her children. Prayer was as necessary as air to breathe, and Charles and John took in deep portions of it.

In the fruitful years of their ministry, prayer was the centerpiece of their work. Because they traveled thousands of miles, mostly on horseback, there were hours to pray. They took time to pray for the converts whose lives and businesses were threatened because of their newfound faith.

For Charles, prayers began to flow freely in musical and verse form. He would meditate on a passage of Scripture and translate it into singable theology for his brother to organize into hymn tracts and books for the common people. The hymnbooks became the weapon of the faith revolution. Even illiterate people could learn a hymn and sing it for encouragement. Every trial they faced had an appropriate biblical hymn text to use to keep despair from overtaking them. Charles's and John's obedience literally fueled a transformation of the culture.

When he was forty years old, Charles penned the hymn "Love Divine, All Loves Excelling" to encourage the troubled converts to focus on the joy of heaven and holy living on earth. Nearly ninety years after Charles's death a tune entitled "Beecher" was written for the lyric by John Zundel, which is familiar to us today.

John Zundel was born in Germany and studied the violin and worked as a bandmaster and organist in Russia. He immigrated to America in 1847 and became the organist at Plymouth Church, Brooklyn, New York. The pastor of the church was Henry Ward Beecher, for whom Zundel named the famous tune.

Elizabeth Payson Prentiss
1818-1878

William Doane
1832-1913

More love to thee, O Christ, more love to thee!
Hear thou the prayer I make on bended knee;
This is my earnest plea, more love, O Christ, to thee,
More love to thee, more love to thee!

Once earthly joy I craved, sought peace and rest;
Now thee alone I seek; give what is best:
This all my prayer shall be, more love, O Christ, to thee,
More love to thee, more love to thee!

Let sorrow do its work, send grief and pain;
Sweet are thy messengers, sweet their refrain,
When they can sing with me, more love, O Christ, to thee,
More love to thee, more love to thee!

Then shall my latest breath whisper thy praise;
This be the parting cry my heart shall raise,
This still its prayer shall be, more love, O Christ, to thee,
More love to thee, more love to thee!

AT THE HEART OF THE HYMN

Robert Wolgemuth

Joseph was still in the house when Judah and his brothers came in, and they threw themselves to the ground before him.

—GENESIS 44:14

I WAS IN HIGH SCHOOL WHEN I first heard the expression *body language*. I can remember the fun we had in Mr. Tate's sociology class, talking about how only a small fraction of communication between two people is carried by words. The majority has to do with facial expressions, how we stand, or what we do with our arms while we are talking.

I remember discussing clues about how we could tell when someone was really listening when we were talking: like smiling, leaning in, tilting the head slightly, nodding, or blinking a lot. And we talked about how we could tell when someone wasn't listening: frowning, shifting eyes, folding the arms, leaning back.

For weeks I looked around the school cafeteria, watching students in conversation. I tried to read clues that they were sending to each other. And I paid special attention to what I did when I was talking to my friends . . . and what they did in return. I was completely taken by all of this.

As a very young boy, my first memories of church included sitting on the second or third row with my mother and three older siblings. She did her best to keep us quiet because she knew that the folks in our church were keeping an eye on us. Noise or distraction coming from our pew wouldn't have reflected well on the credibility of the minister. Our pastor was also our dad.

There were no musical instruments in the church. When we'd sing a hymn, all we heard were voices. Mother sang a strong, sweet soprano, and we learned the fun of harmonizing with her.

I loved this hymn. We often sang it at the close of the service as an invitation and benediction. And I remember what a few of the people did during the singing.

Very inconspicuously some of the worshipers lifted their hands in the air. They weren't showing off. They were simply putting themselves in a position that spoke of their love for God, their awe at the idea of being in His presence and singing to His glory. It was spiritual body language.

When my dad called for the congregation to pray, he would step back from the pulpit and kneel down beside it. We would stand, turn around, and kneel down at the pews, our knees resting on the hardwood floor and our elbows barely reaching the bench. Dad never had to remind us that we were bringing our praise and our petitions before the living God. Our kneeling said it all—more spiritual body language.

And my dad didn't leave his kneeling at the church. Very early every morning we were wakened by the sound of his praying downstairs. We couldn't make out any words, but the resonance of his deep voice quietly reverberated through the house. And we knew that he was on his knees.

Over the years I have had the fun of visiting some of the world's most majestic churches: Westminster Abbey in London, St. Patrick's Church in New York City, Trinity Episcopal in Boston, and Grace Cathedral in San Francisco. All these churches have something in common—they have kneelers. In addition to knowing how to design breathtaking structures, the architects knew something about the body language of the people. When it's time to pray, parishioners go to their knees.

Like many historic anthems of the church, this hymn is a powerful prayer. It includes challenging words that deal with our priorities—"Once earthly joy I craved . . . now thee alone I seek." It embraces suffering—"Let sorrow do its work, send grief and pain." It speaks of death—"Then shall my latest breath whisper thy praise."

But this hymn does what my dad did. It does what those great architects did. This hymn reminds us not only of what we should say to the Father, but what our body language ought to be.

Hear thou the prayer I make
On bended knee.

In the Light of the Word

John MacArthur

This precious hymn is a prayer. It begins with the recognition that only divine grace can enable our hearts to love God in the first place. Scripture clearly teaches this. "The sinful mind is hostile to God. It does not submit to God's law, nor can it do so. Those controlled by the sinful nature cannot please God" (Romans 8:7-8). So unless God Himself draws us to Christ, we would never love Him on our own (John 6:65). "We love because he first loved us" (1 John 4:19).

The apostle Paul prayed for the Philippians, "And this is my prayer: that your love may abound more and more in knowledge and depth of insight" (Philippians 1:9). So it is certainly appropriate to pray that God would deepen and enrich our love for Christ, for only He can do it.

Elizabeth Prentiss, who wrote this hymn, was severely disabled by constant pain for most of her life. She wrote this hymn during a time of deep grief after two of her children died in infancy very close together. Her "earnest plea" in the midst of such overwhelming trials was not that the trials would be removed or that the pain would be eliminated, but that patience would have its perfect work: "that you may be mature and complete, not lacking anything" (James 1:4). That is the heart-cry of true faith.

Stanza 2 is a beautiful testimony that describes how trials refine the believer's perspective: "Once earthly joy I craved." Joy is certainly a legitimate expression of spiritual fruit (Galatians 5:22). We are even commanded to be joyful in the midst of our trials (James 1:2). But this is not a mere *earthly* joy. Earthly joys are always temporary and transient. And yet those are the kinds of joy most people spend their lives in pursuit of.

The testimony of the hymn-writer is that Christ Himself is a blessing vastly superior to any earthly joy, and that is where the sorrowful heart finally learns to find its *true* joy: "Now thee alone I seek."

Vance Havner borrowed that line as the title of a famous sermon he preached shortly after his wife died. He spoke passionately about the difficulties of adjusting to life alone and coping with excruciating grief after the Lord took the love of his life home to heaven. And he said that in the midst of all his pain and heartache, one great blessing was sustaining him: His love for Christ meant more to him than ever, and he was focused like never before on the pursuit of that love. He learned to cope with earthly grief by cultivating a greater measure of heavenly love for Christ.

That is precisely what the hymn-writer had in mind. Stanza 3 actually embraces the "sorrow," "grief," and "pain" of earthly trials—not out of some kind of masochistic love of hurting, but because of the joyous spiritual fruit borne in the midst of such trials. That is the very truth James was speaking about when he wrote, "Consider it *pure joy*, my brothers, whenever you face trials of many kinds, because you know that the testing of your faith develops perseverance" (James 1:2- 3, emphasis added).

The hymn poetically echoes the message of James 1: "Sweet are thy messengers." Remember, the "messengers" the hymn-writer has in mind are "sorrow," "grief," and "pain." Again, these are in no way "sweet" in and of themselves. But when their effects on our hearts actually increase our love and our longing for Christ, the final result *is* unspeakably sweet. Thus the sweetest songs often grow out of the bitterest experiences (and this hymn is a classic example of that). If we allow our trials to turn our hearts toward Christ, the final "refrain" of all our sufferings will be like the refrain of this hymn: "More love O Christ, to thee, more love to thee, more love to thee!"

The closing stanza looks forward to the end of life, realizing that a prayer like this hymn is never fully answered this side of heaven. No matter how deep and rich our love for Christ grows in this life, we will always feel the need for deeper, more perfect love. And that will be true until the moment when we see Him face to face and are made perfect (1 John 3:2). Then even our love for our glorious Savior will finally be perfect, and the prayer of this hymn will at last be answered in full.

From Out of the Past

Bobbie Wolgemuth

From the time she was a young girl, Elizabeth Payson Prentiss captured American readers with her poetry, stories, and articles in widely read youth magazines published in Boston and New York. And it's not surprising that a hymn that embraces deepest devotion to Christ came from the pen of a tenderhearted woman who suffered unthinkable grief.

Her love of children was evident in her writing. Born in Maine, she grew up in the home of a minister and was no stranger to the love of Scripture. In her late twenties she fell in love with a young theological student named George Lewis Prentiss. They were married the same year he became pastor of a church in New Bedford, Massachusetts, and Elizabeth became a schoolteacher. It wasn't long until she had her own children to write stories for, and motherhood afforded a firsthand look at home and hearth for her many children's books.

The couple moved to New York City, where George was installed as pastor of a Presbyterian church. The work of moving and setting up their new home did not keep Elizabeth from continuing to write. The Little Susy Library series and volumes of her captivating stories were published. Then the young minister and his wife faced the devastation of losing one of their children, and with no time for a grieving mother and father to heal, their youngest child also died. But tragedy did not stop Elizabeth from writing.

With grief as deep as her tender heart could stand, she poured her aches onto the pages of her journal. She wrote of "empty hands, a worn-out, exhausted body, and unutterable longings to flee from a world that has so many sharp experiences." Instead of blaming God for her loss, she ran into His open arms in prose, content to view her pain as a "sweet messenger." She wrote, "One child and two green graves are mine, this is God's gift to me." She promised to give her "fainting, broken heart" as a gift back to her heavenly Father.

From the crucible of anguish came the prayer verse that would become the beloved hymn "More Love to Thee, O Christ."

Elizabeth was meditating on Scripture and Sarah Adams's hymn "Nearer, My God, to Thee" one evening when all four verses of "More Love to Thee, O Christ" completed themselves in her mind as a personal prayer. So intimate was the experience that she did not even show what she had written to her husband. Cringing at the idea that these verses would bring any praise to anyone but her Savior alone, she would not think of offering the words to any of her publishers either. It was thirteen years later, when she showed the text to her husband, that they decided to share it with the world.

In her fifties, Elizabeth published a fictional journal of a nineteenth-century girl entitled *Stepping Heavenward* that had enormous sales in America and was translated into many languages. Drawing on the riches of her own experiences in childhood and as a young adult, she was the kind of storyteller that captured the hearts of readers worldwide.

William Doane, who also wrote the popular tunes for "To God Be the Glory" and "Near the Cross," wrote the music for "More Love to Thee, O Christ." He was a successful businessman who composed over two thousand hymn tunes and published numerous hymn collections. His successful manufacturing ventures and inventions afforded him the money to buy a pipe organ for a YMCA hall in Ohio and to construct a music building in Chicago. Known as an unselfish benefactor, William generously gave time and money to many civic and church causes. Like Elizabeth, he was motivated to share all he had to show his love for Christ.

FANNY CROSBY
1820-1915

ROBERT LOWRY
1826-1899

All the way my Savior leads me; what have I to ask beside?
Can I doubt his tender mercy, who through life has been my guide?
Heav'nly peace, divinest comfort, here by faith in him to dwell;
For I know, whate'er befall me, Jesus doeth all things well;
For I know, whate'er befall me, Jesus doeth all things well.

All the way my Savior leads me, cheers each winding path I tread,
Gives me grace for ev'ry trial, feeds me with the living bread.
Though my weary steps may falter, and my soul athirst may be,
Gushing from the rock before me, lo, a spring of joy I see;
Gushing from the rock before me, lo, a spring of joy I see.

All the way my Savior leads me—O the fulness of his love!
Perfect rest to me is promised in my Father's house above:
When my spirit, clothed, immortal, wings its flight to realms of day,
This my song through endless ages: Jesus led me all the way;
This my song through endless ages: Jesus led me all the way!

At the Heart of the Hymn

Robert Wolgemuth

Even though I walk through the valley of the shadow of death, I will fear no evil, for you are with me.

—Psalm 23:4

"How long until we get there, Daddy?"

Early in our parenting days Bobbie and I tried to avoid this question from the backseat at all costs. We lived in Chicago, and Bobbie's parents lived in Washington, DC. The trip took about twelve hours by car, but for a small child it might as well have taken two weeks. There are only so many things you can do to keep a three-year-old and a six-year-old occupied.

So we decided to take the trip at night. As I put the finishing touches on packing the suitcases into our car, Bobbie was outfitting the girls in their pajamas. Some pillows, quilts, and the girls' favorite blankets turned the backseat into a bed. The drudgery of a long trip was going to become a great adventure.

With a few songs and bedtime prayers under our belts, we headed east on the Tri-State Tollway. By the time we hit the Indiana Turnpike, Missy and Julie, with the sun behind us, had pulled the covers up for a good night's sleep. We headed into the darkness, looking forward to reaching Ray and Gerry Gardner's northern Virginia home. Grandpa and Grandma were waiting for us.

Bobbie always did her best to stay awake, but by the time we reached the Goshen, Indiana, exit, she wasn't much for conversation. My gas tank was only a quarter down, but my wife, "the shotgun," was empty, if you know what I mean. "Are you okay, honey?" she'd say every once in a while over the next several hours. She'd awaken long enough to make sure I wasn't dozing off.

"I'm fine," I'd answer, happy with the companionship of my coffee Thermos and a steady stream of eighteen-wheelers.

At the Breezewood exit on the Pennsylvania Turnpike, we turned south toward Maryland and Washington. And by the time our car merged onto the Beltway, the barely detectable morning glow to my left signaled the dawn of a new day. We were almost home.

Turning our car down the long tree-lined driveway in Alexandria, I let out a long sigh. Bobbie woke up. "Can I drive for a while?" she said, stretching her cramped legs against the floorboard.

"Sure, honey," I said with a smile. "We've only made it to your parents' driveway. Why don't you take it on in from here."

We both laughed quietly, not wanting to waken the girls.

Our headlights sweeping across the front yard signaled our arrival. Dad and Mother came down the sidewalk and, after some welcoming hugs, helped us carry suitcases into the house. One at a time I gently lifted the girls from the backseat and carried them into the room Grandma had lovingly prepared for them. Laying them down on clean soft sheets, I pulled the covers up to their chins and kissed their foreheads.

One night earlier they had fallen asleep speeding eastward on I-94, and soon they'd wake up in a new, yet wonderfully familiar place. The loving sound of Grandma and Grandpa's voices would quicken their hearts.

On February 5, 2002, at about 2:30 in the afternoon, my precious dad fell asleep. His life had been filled with love for his wife and family. He had been faithful and obedient to God's call. As a young Lancaster County farm boy, Samuel Wolgemuth had followed the Savior's leading and ministered around the world. He and our mother had raised six children. We had presented them with twenty grandchildren and thirteen great-grandchildren.

And then, completely exhausted from the rigors and demands of life—and plenty of good-bye hymns and prayers—Dad had closed his eyes.

The next thing my dad saw was the dawn of another day—in a new, yet wonderfully familiar place. The Father had gently carried him from his bedroom to a place even more exquisite than he could have ever imagined.

Dad had fallen asleep on the journey, and in what seemed like just a moment, he awakened in a place where the sheets were soft and the welcome unmatched by anything he had ever known. The drudgery of a long trip had become a great adventure. The Savior had gently lifted his weakened body and carried him to the place his Father had lovingly prepared for him. The voices of old friends quickened his heart. But the face of Jesus filled him with joy like he had never known.

The journey had ended. At last my dad was home.

Perfect rest to me is promised in
my Father's house above . . .
This my song through endless ages;
Jesus led me all the way.

In the Light of the Word

John MacArthur

This is a beautiful expression of faith and personal testimony, celebrating the abundant sufficiency of Christ. The first line is a strong echo of the first verse of the familiar Twenty-Third Psalm: "The Lord is my shepherd, I shall not be in want." With Christ as our guide through life, how could we ever imagine that we were lacking anything necessary? "In [Him] are hidden all the treasures of wisdom and knowledge" (Colossians 2:3). All the fullness of God dwells in Him (Colossians 1:19). "God will meet all [our] needs according to his glorious riches in Christ Jesus" (Philippians 4:19).

And we can be perfectly content with what we have, because He has said, "Never will I leave you; never will I forsake you" (Hebrews 13:5). In the songwriter's words, "What have I to ask beside?"

The second line then asks, "Can I doubt his tender mercy, who through life has been my guide?" The Lord's "tender mercy" is a constant theme in Scripture. The expression is borrowed from the King James Version. Most modern versions use the word *compassion* instead. But there is a strong note of gentleness and warm affection in the expression "tender mercy" that I prefer.

The Hebrew word translated "tender mercies" throughout the King James Version of the Old Testament is a feminine expression that refers to the internal organs, and specifically the womb. It portrays God's tender compassion as that which envelops us in absolute security and loving nurture, like a fetus inside the womb. Even in the midst of life's harshest trials and tragedies, we are surrounded and protected by an impenetrable shelter of divine compassion and care, so that we are eternally safe in His perfect care.

That security is what gives us a sense of "heav'nly peace, divinest comfort." In other words, it is a taste of heaven on earth. But as the songwriter notes, such a sense of security, and the peace that attends it, can be laid hold of only "by faith in him."

And in the midst of life's difficulties, we may rest in the promise that our lives are governed by a loving, sovereign Providence. Christ knows what He is doing, and He is doing it for our good. As the multitudes who were overwhelmed with amazement at the ministry of Christ testified, "He has done everything well" (Mark 7:37).

In the closing line of the first stanza, the songwriter surely has in mind one of the most beloved promises of Scripture, Romans 8:28: "We know that in all things God works for the good of those who love him, who have been called according to his purpose." "All things" work together for our good, because the One who does "all things" well is the same One who sovereignly superintends every aspect of our lives. He allows no temptation to overtake us that is sufficient to destroy us (1 Corinthians 10:13); He shields us by His power (1 Peter 1:5); and He works everything for our good. He "doeth all things well."

The second stanza develops the imagery suggested by the Twenty-Third Psalm. The Great Shepherd accompanies us, sustains us, and feeds us as He watches over us. He "cheers each winding path" by the sheer comfort of His unfaltering presence (Hebrews 13:5); He gives abundant "grace for every trial" (James 4:6; 2 Corinthians 12:9); and He feeds us "with the living bread" (John 6:51).

The closing line of that second stanza ("Gushing from the rock before me, lo! a spring of joy I see!") is a reference to the incident in Exodus 17, where Moses smote the rock in the wilderness, and out of that rock came enough water to quench the thirst of all the Israelites. Even in the stark, arid barrenness of the desert, that rock could become a source of abundant provision under the hand of Almighty God. Thus it is even with our trial-filled lives. Christ is able to lead us to abundant sources of joy no matter how difficult our circumstances.

The final stanza looks forward to the heavenly glory that lies at the end of the pathway of suffering (cf. Romans 8:18). When we reach that "perfect rest," we will celebrate forever the fact that Christ is the one who led us there, and all the glory will be His for all eternity.

From Out of the Past

Bobbie Wolgemuth

Frances Jane Crosby was the sweet-singing blind girl who became America's most loved hymn-writer. Blinded as an infant, she was able only to distinguish light from darkness. But her courage and cheerfulness transformed the tragedy into "God's greatest gift to my life." And her personality was so full of light that she saw herself as the "happiest creature in all the land."

Before Fanny was a year old, her father, a farmer, died suddenly. Her devoted mother hired herself out as a maid, and her grandmother was left with the task of training Fanny. Her grandmother took her on long nature walks, where even colors of flowers were described in vivid detail. From the word pictures painted by her grandmother, Fanny chose the violet as her favorite flower.

For hours every day her grandmother read long passages from the Bible to Fanny. This foundation of Scripture set her on a course to change the world. Fanny saw her handicap as a doorway to reach her goal—that her life would be the means of bringing one million people to Christ.

As a youngster, Fanny loved to pray, and from those prayers she experienced many answers. The most important was for a proper education. Fanny and her grandmother knelt together, asking God for a specific answer to her prayer. The answer came in November 1834 when her mother read aloud a circular that told of the first United States School for the Blind that was opening in New York City. Fanny described that day as "the happiest day of her life."

The Braille system had not yet been recognized, but the institute provided study in languages, English, history, and music by reading out loud and lecturing. Considering her ability to memorize to be one of her greatest gifts, Fanny took top honors in all her classes. And she became accomplished in piano and guitar and gave concerts on the harp and organ.

It was another answer to prayer that inspired the writing of the hymn, "All the Way My Savior Leads Me." On one occasion she was in need of some money. She humbly sought God for the provision, telling Him the specific amount she needed. Within a few minutes there was a knock on her door. When she opened it a stranger handed her some money—the exact amount she had requested. "I have no way of accounting for this, except to believe that God put it into the heart of this good man to bring the money," she later wrote. "It is so wonderful the way the Lord leads me."

Fanny continued to write, speak, and sing until the last years before her death at age ninety-five. Having written over nine thousand hymns and verses that had intimately touched hearts, her funeral was a display of love from thousands. People stood in line for blocks to honor her. At her service each person in the congregation was given a violet, which they dropped as they filed by her casket to surround the sweet singer of hymns with a bed of violets.

Dr. Robert Lowry set the verses of this hymn to music. A gifted pastor who spent hours studying hymnology and composing in his spare time, he saw hymns as the Gospel clothed in singable tunes. Dr. Lowry compiled and published several songbooks, many for use with children in Sunday school. Fanny made a significant contribution to songbooks he compiled. To avoid having her name appear too many times, she used over 200 pen names. It did not matter to either Dr. Lowry or Fanny who received the credit, as long as the hymns were sung and people's hearts were touched.

Reginald Heber
1783-1826

John B. Dykes
1823-1876

Holy, holy, holy! Lord God Almighty!
Early in the morning our song shall rise to thee.
Holy, holy, holy! Merciful and mighty!
God in three Persons, blessed Trinity!

Holy, holy, holy! All the saints adore thee,
Casting down their golden crowns around the glassy sea;
Cherubim and seraphim falling down before thee,
Who wert, and art, and evermore shalt be.

Holy, holy, holy! Though the darkness hide thee,
Though the eye of sinful man thy glory may not see,
Only thou art holy; there is none beside thee
Perfect in pow'r, in love, and purity.

Holy, holy, holy! Lord God Almighty!
All thy works shall praise thy name in earth and sky and sea.
Holy, holy, holy! Merciful and mighty!
God in three Persons, blessed Trinity!

At the Heart of the Hymn

Robert Wolgemuth

"Holy, holy, holy is the Lord God Almighty, who was, and is, and is to come."

—Revelation 4:8b

The great hymns of the church are great because they are brimming with great theology—even when you're too young to understand it. Just ask Abby.

Living in central Florida has some wonderful benefits. The weather is terrific year-round, and there are more things to see than you can imagine. Out-of-town friends often come by to see us. It's great. But the best part of living here is that our home is like a huge magnet, and our grandchildren are like little helpless metal shavings.

Of course, they would love to visit Nanny and Granddaddy anyway, but these extra things make our place irresistible!

A while ago Abigail Grace, our oldest grandchild, spent two weeks with us. At the time she was five years old, and with all due respect to her parents, she didn't get homesick at all. There was too much going on around here to even have a tinge of that.

One of the things that both Bobbie and our daughter Missy, Abby's mother, have determined to do is to teach the children some of the great hymns, right along with many of the newer praise songs and choruses. On this particular visit to Florida, the hymn of choice was "Holy, Holy, Holy!"

Because Bobbie can make a game out of almost anything, she decided to combine time in the swimming pool with memorizing the lyrics to the song. They'd sit on the step at one end of the pool, and Bobbie would rehearse a phrase. Then Abby would swim to the other end and back, repeating the line she had just learned.

"Holy, holy, holy! Lord God Almighty," Abby gasped as she splashed her way to the far end of the pool. "Early in the morning our song shall rise to thee." Undaunted by some unscheduled gulping of a little chlorinated water, Abby coughed out, "Holy, holy, holy! Merciful and mighty! God in three Persons, blessed Trinity."

When she paddled back to Nanny, she repeated the phrase, and they celebrated. It was quite a sight.

By the third day they were making their way through the second verse. Over a lunch of cheese sandwiches and lemonade, I got the lowdown. "All the saints adore thee," Abby recited. "Casting down their golden crowns around the glassy sea."

I remembered teaching through the book of Revelation many years before and how the apostle John had seen a vision of these wonderful things—creatures of every description falling down before the One who sat on the throne.

"Cherubim and seraphim falling down before thee." I have images of these two kinds of creatures in my mind, but I always forget which is which. Then a thought crossed my mind. *Does this five-year-old have any idea what seraphim are? Shouldn't we simplify these concepts for her?*

"Who wert, and art, and evermore shalt be," Abby said between bites of her sandwich, proudly finishing the second verse.

"Do you think we should change these words into something she understands?" I asked Bobbie.

"No," she replied without hesitating. "I've already thought it through. These truths are like little mysterious seeds quietly tucked away in Abby's heart. Someday they'll grow, and then she'll understand what they mean. They'll provide her with one of the greatest truths in the Bible."

I knew Bobbie was right.

God is holy and eternal. He was with us in our yesterdays. He is here right now. And when we get to tomorrow—whatever and wherever that may be—He will be there waiting for us.

That afternoon, as Abby pummeled the water on her way from one end of the pool to the other, I could hear her repeat these incredible words of comfort and assurance: "Who wert, and art, and evermore shalt be."

She successfully reached the far end of the pool and looked up at me with great delight. "I made it, Granddaddy," Abby said to me. "I made it to the other side."

I laughed out loud and clapped my celebration. "Good girl, Abby," I said. "I'm so proud of you."

She smiled back at me, thinking I was talking about her ability to swim.

Worthy are you, our Lord and God, to receive glory and honor and power. . . .

—REVELATION 4:11A, ESV

IN THE LIGHT OF THE WORD
John MacArthur

THIS STATELY HYMN CELEBRATES the Trinity. It is based on the apostle John's vision of God's throne, in which he saw four angelic beings hovering around the throne of God day and night, saying, "Holy, holy, holy is the Lord God Almighty, who was, and is, and is to come" (Revelation 4:8). The prophet Isaiah saw a similar vision, and he recorded how he heard the seraphs (angelic beings) worshiping God by calling to one another with these words: "Holy, holy, holy is the Lord Almighty; the whole earth is full of his glory" (Isaiah 6:3).

The threefold repetition of the word *holy* reminded hymn-writer Reginald Heber of the three Persons of God. So he borrowed those words as the theme for this classic Trinitarian hymn.

The hymn is filled with scriptural references. The phrase "early in the morning our song shall rise to thee," for example, is a reference to Psalm 5:3: "In the morning, O LORD, you hear my voice; in the morning I lay my requests before you and wait in expectation." Psalm 63:1 in the King James Version says, "O God, thou art my God; early will I seek thee." Scripture thus repeatedly portrays the eagerness of the true believer who arises to worship God "early in the morning."

Many of the biblical allusions in the hymn are borrowed from Revelation 4 and John's description of his heavenly vision. A phrase in the second stanza, "casting down their golden crowns," is a reference to Revelation 4:10: "The four and twenty elders fall down before him that sat on the throne, and worship him that liveth for ever and ever, and cast their crowns before the throne" (KJV). The "glassy sea" alludes to verse 6 (KJV): "Before the throne there was a sea of glass like unto crystal."

The picture of those elders in Revelation 4:10 falling down before the throne of God no doubt inspired the phrase at the end of the second stanza, "falling down before thee." That is further echoed in several more passages in the book of Revelation where human and angelic beings ("cherubim and seraphim") fall on their faces before the throne of God: "All the angels were standing around the throne and around the elders and the four living creatures. They fell down on their faces before the throne and worshiped God" (Revelation 7:11). "And the twenty-four elders, who were seated on their thrones before God, fell on their faces and worshiped God" (11:16). "The twenty-four elders and the four living creatures fell down and worshiped God, who was seated on the throne. And they cried: 'Amen, Hallelujah!'" (Revelation 19:4).

The phrase "Who wert, and art, and evermore shalt be" sounds somewhat archaic to twenty-first-century ears, but it is another reference to the verse that inspired this hymn, Revelation 4:8: "Holy, holy, holy is the Lord God Almighty, *who was, and is, and is to come*" (emphasis added). Revelation 1:4 also refers to God as "him who is, and who was, and who is to come." Verse 8 repeats the expression: "'I am the Alpha and the Omega,' says the Lord God, 'who is, and who was, and who is to come, the Almighty.'" Those names all emphasize the constancy and immutability of God and of Jesus Christ, "the same yesterday and today and forever" (Hebrews 13:8).

The first line of the third stanza says, "though the darkness hide thee." That is probably an oblique reference to how God appeared to the Israelites at the foot of Mount Sinai. A supernatural darkness caused fear to fall upon the people, and Scripture records, "The people remained at a distance, while Moses approached the thick darkness where God was" (Exodus 20:21).

Yet while God may at times *appear* to be hidden in darkness, in reality, He "lives in unapproachable light, whom no one has seen or can see" (1 Timothy 6:16). It is only "the eye of sinful man" that cannot see His glory (cf. Exodus 33:20).

The final stanza includes yet another reference to Scripture. Psalm 145:10 in the King James Version says, "All thy works shall praise thee, O Lord; and thy saints shall bless thee."

I love the juxtaposition of the words "merciful and mighty" in the first and last stanzas of this hymn. Some might think those attributes are incongruous. In God, they both exist in absolute perfection and consummate harmony. He is *both* merciful and mighty—and that is why He sent His Son to be our Savior.

From Out of the Past

Bobbie Wolgemuth

Bookcases full of masterpieces and rare books filled the extensive library in the boyhood home of Reginald Heber. His wealthy and cultured English parents gave Reginald a love of the finest literature and poetic genius of the day. The Bible was held in highest regard in his home. He learned stories and Scripture from infancy. By the time he was five years old, he could give chapter and verse for random quotations. He was just seven years old when he translated a Latin classic into English verse.

His hunger for words and love of Scripture shaped his youthful mind and personality. Reginald was such a generous lad that when he went away to a boarding school his parents had to sew his money into the pocket lining of his coat so he would not give it away in charity before the semester was over.

He entered Oxford University when he was seventeen and won prizes for his

Latin and English poetry. But the laurel that meant the most to him was awarded at his college commencement exercises. He received overwhelming applause and exceptional praise for a poem he had written called "Palestine." The humble graduate did not forget to thank God. His mother, looking for him after the ceremony, softly opened the door of his dorm room to find Reginald on his knees in thanksgiving.

After graduation, twenty-four-year-old Reginald became minister in his hometown, where he served a congregation with creativity and excellence for over sixteen years. Singing was first on the list of improvements he wanted for his assembly, who had been accustomed to metrical psalmody. He wanted hymnbooks to be placed at each seat in the pew. None were available, so he resolved to put together a hymnal of his own and invited his friends to contribute. With elegance and brilliant literary form, he adorned and interpreted the Bible in verse form.

The most prized hymn that Reginald Heber gave to the congregation was "Holy, Holy, Holy!" Even today, no hymn has greater dignity and liturgical weight.

Adjacent to the church, he built a stately brick home with his own means and planned an extensive garden and grounds with magnificent trees. This is where he sat for hours creating his sermons and powerful and memorable word-pictures. The loveliness of the sight crept into the hymns that have become the world's delight.

When Reginald was forty, he traveled with his wife and two small children to India as a missionary. Years before he had written the best known of missionary hymns, "From Greenland's Icy Mountains." His passion for world missions was evident, and the hymn promoted the missionary cause throughout Protestant circles.

He was appointed Bishop of Calcutta. In addition to days filled with ceaseless labor, the hot, humid climate of India took its toll on the whole family. Reginald described the weather as a "hot and molten atmosphere, which streams in like the breath of a huge blast furnace." Such a day was the one that would be his last when he was only forty-two years old.

Reginald was scheduled to preach in a mission chapel in the morning, but the crowd that came to hear him was so large that he moved outside to speak from the steps of the mission house. He suffered sunstroke and by afternoon returned to his friends' house where he died. He had spent his last day on earth doing what he had been called to. This is most eloquently stated in his own missionary hymn: "Salvation! O salvation! The joyful sound proclaim, till earth's remotest nation has learned Messiah's name."

One of England's leading church musicians, Dr. John Dykes, wrote the tune that fits so perfectly with the text for "Holy, Holy, Holy!" Dykes entitled the tune "Nicaea." It was in the first church Council of Nicaea in Asia Minor in A.D. 325 that the doctrine of the Trinity was clearly defined and determined to be an essential belief of the Christian faith. John Dykes found the musical match in thought and spirit for the poetic expression of the Trinity. Because of this song's uplifting power in word and song, no hymn is greater.

WILLIAM O. CUSHING
1823-1903

GEORGE ROOT
1820-1895

When he cometh, when he cometh to make up his jewels,
All his jewels, precious jewels, his loved and his own.

Refrain:
Like the stars of the morning, his bright crown adorning,
They shall shine in their beauty, bright gems for his crown.

He will gather, he will gather the gems for his kingdom,
All the pure ones, all the bright ones, his loved and his own.

Little children, little children who love their Redeemer,
Are the jewels, precious jewels, his loved and his own.

At the Heart of the Hymn

Joni Eareckson Tada

The LORD their God will save them on that day as the flock of his people.
They will sparkle in his land like jewels in a crown.

—ZECHARIAH 9:16

NOT FAR FROM THE FARM where I grew up was a stone quarry called Sylvan Dell. When we would ride our horses on the nearby bridle path, we were careful to stay on the trail. That's because not twenty feet from the path a sheer cliff plunged to the bottom of the quarry. Sylvan Dell was always busy. Steam shovels and trucks moved huge rocks that eventually became flagstone for the new housing developments that were springing up near the farm. The quarry was a place of noise, hammering, and clouds of dust.

Years later when Sylvan Dell began to fill with water from an underground spring, the trucks and steam shovels left. The area became utterly quiet. You could even hear birds calling in the woods—something unheard of when the quarry was up and running.

During a recent visit home, we drove down Old Court Road, which still borders Sylvan Dell, so I could see some of the old bridle paths. We pulled over at the entrance to the quarry where ivy and weeds covered the gate. We sat and listened to the silence. A whippoorwill called in the woods. Peace and quiet enveloped us.

Sometime later when I got back home, I thought about Sylvan Dell when I stumbled across 1 Kings 6:7: "In building the temple, only blocks dressed at the quarry were used, and no hammer, chisel or any other iron tool was heard at the temple site while it was being built." The temple of God was a place of utter quiet and serenity. All the hammering and chiseling was done at the quarry and *not* at the temple site.

First Peter 2:5 says we are "living stones"—we are being "dressed" in the quarry of earth, a place of noise, hammering, chiseling, and clouds of dust. We get steam-shoveled by suffering, and affliction jars us like a jackhammer. Yet God is using pain and heartache to hone and shape us so we will fit perfectly into heaven's landscape. A place where there is "no hammer, chisel or any other iron tool." Where there is no suffering. No tears, pain, sorrow, or death.

As polished stones, not only will we fit in heaven, we will fit as glittering jewels in His crown. Friend, you and I aren't ordinary flagstone in the household of faith; no, we are living stones destined to be jewels. We have reason to rejoice. Soon we will enter the utter serenity of heaven—a place of peace and quiet—and God will set us in His diadem as sparkling and dazzling jewels!

Now this begs the question: who are the brightest jewels? Who are the ones who will *really* shine? The answer is found in Matthew 20:26-28: ". . . whoever wants to become great among you must be your servant, and whoever wants to be first must be your slave—just as the Son of Man did not come to be served, but to serve, and to give his life as a ransom for many." They say that when you are going through hard times, when you're facing hardship and affliction, the best thing you can do is to help someone else with their problems. If you want to be first in the kingdom—if you wish to one day sparkle like a jewel in a crown—then don't focus on the hammer, dust, and chisel in your own life, but look to the hardships of others. Help them. Serve them. And you will be set as a prominent jewel in God's crown. You will be most fitting!

My most recent visit to Sylvan Dell revealed that the bridle path around the quarry can hardly be located through the thicket. Not so with the quarry of God. He's as active as ever, mining out more living stones every day. He's also busy with His hammer and chisel, honing and shaping us to sparkle and shine. True, it's painful; in Zechariah 13:9 He says, "I will refine them like silver and test them like gold." But take heart. He has a crown in mind for you.

So bear a bit longer with the noise and hammering. Serve and help others as you wait. It's the jewel thing to do.

In the Light of the Word

John MacArthur

This is a short, modest hymn about the return of Christ. It is a song of simple faith, especially for children. It avoids all the typical arguments about various eschatological schemes and simply focuses on the main point: the fact of Jesus' return for His chosen ones.

The words are based on Malachi 3:16-17 in the King James Version: "Then they that feared the Lord spake often one to another: and the Lord hearkened, and heard it, and a book of remembrance was written before him for them that feared the Lord, and that thought upon his name. They shall be mine, saith the Lord of hosts, in that day when I make up my jewels; and I will spare them, as a man spareth his own son that serveth him."

That passage speaks of God's love for His own chosen ones. It is comparable to the love of a father for his son; so when the Lord speaks of *sparing* those who fear Him "just as in compassion a man spares his son who serves him" (NIV), He is speaking about sparing them from judgment.

The original text from Malachi is a prophecy about the return of Christ in His glory. The purpose of His coming is twofold: On the one hand, there will be severe judgment for those who do not fear the Lord; and on the other hand, Christ will gather together His people as a man gently handles a precious treasure. The word translated "jewels" in the King James Version actually means "special treasure." So in the NIV, verse 17 is translated this way: "'They will be mine,' says the LORD Almighty, 'in the day when I make up my treasured possession.'"

Our song uses the idea of jewels, however, and it is fitting imagery to capture the sense of Malachi's prophecy. The treasured possession, "his jewels," speaks of *His people*. The hymn, written as a didactic tool for children, doesn't reveal that fact until the final stanza. The first two stanzas speak of His coming to "gather the gems for his kingdom" (stanza 2). We know that they are "jewels, precious jewels, his loved and his own." They are radiant in their glory: "Like the stars of the morning." They are ornaments for His diadem: "his bright crown adorning . . . bright gems for his crown." But not until the closing stanza do we discover *what* these gems are: "Little children, little children, who love their Redeemer."

That is a fine description of all true believers, because Jesus said in Mark 10:15 and Luke 18:17, "Anyone who will not receive the kingdom of God like a little child will never enter it." He did not mean, of course, that people must come to faith in their childhood in order to be saved. Rather, He was saying that true saving faith is childlike. In the words of Matthew 18:3, "Unless you change and become like little children, you will never enter the kingdom of heaven." And the rest of Matthew 18 goes on to describe several ways in which all true believers' faith is childlike.

A jewel perfectly symbolizes the believer in glory. In the first place, believers have *priceless value*, because "it was not with perishable things such as silver or gold that you were redeemed . . . but with the precious blood of Christ, a lamb without blemish or defect" (1 Peter 1:18-19). Their value is not an intrinsic value, for they were helpless sinners before Christ redeemed them. But they are valuable because God set His love on them and redeemed them at such a high price (cf. Matthew 10:31).

Like jewels, their beauty comes from reflecting bright light from another source. Christ is the embodiment of that light (John 8:12; Revelation 21:23).

The variety of colors in jewels (cf. Revelation 21:18-21) is reminiscent of the diversity among believers. We all have differing gifts (Romans 12:6), different personality types, different cultural and national backgrounds (Revelation 5:9), and other differences of many kinds, but we all are one in Christ (Colossians 3:11).

And our role in eternity will be to reflect God's glory and to worship him, like ornaments in His crown. That is the very imagery captured so well in this exquisite little hymn for children.

FROM OUT OF THE PAST

Paul T. Plew

WILLIAM CUSHING WAS A PASTOR for more than twenty years. Following the death of his wife, he was forced to retire because of his own poor health. As paralysis and loss of speech began to affect his body he prayed, "Lord, give me something to do for Thee."

His prayer was answered; he seemed to have the gift of writing simple Sunday school-style texts. With the encouragement of gospel musicians Ira Sankey and George Root, Cushing wrote over three hundred gospel hymn texts.

"When He Cometh, When He Cometh," sometimes called "The Jewels Song," has been a favorite among children for many years. Cushing wrote it in 1856 for the youth of his church.

Little children, little children who love their Redeemer,
Are the jewels, precious jewels, his loved and his own.

George Frederick Root was organist at Park Street Church in Boston. He studied music for a time under Lowell Mason, who is often referred to as the "Father of Music Education." Mason himself wrote over seven hundred hymns.

After his musical studies were complete, Root moved to New York City, where he taught at the Institute for the Blind. The great hymn-writer Fanny Crosby was one of his students.

Even though Root enjoyed writing secular and patriotic songs, his passion was for writing simple gospel songs. He wrote hundreds of such tunes and helped publish seventy-five collections of songs. It is interesting to see how God brought people together to give songs to the church.

It is said that Root adapted the tune for "When He Cometh, When He Cometh" from a popular post-Civil War melody called "Johnny Schmoker." William Cushing's text was a perfect complement to George Root's music, and the hymn soon became well-known both in Europe and America. Despite language differences, the familiar "Jewel" tune seemed to bind people together in a common tongue.

JOSEPH HENRY GILMORE
1834-1918

WILLIAM BATCHELDER BRADBURY
1816-1868

He leadeth me: O blessed thought!
O words with heav'nly comfort fraught!
Whate'er I do, where'er I be,
Still 'tis God's hand that leadeth me.

Refrain:
He leadeth me, he leadeth me; by his own hand he leadeth me;
His faithful foll'wer I would be, for by his hand he leadeth me.

Sometimes 'mid scenes of deepest gloom,
Sometimes where Eden's bowers bloom,
By waters calm, o'er troubled sea,
Still 'tis his hand that leadeth me.

Lord, I would clasp thy hand in mine,
Nor ever murmur nor repine;
Content, whatever lot I see,
Since 'tis my God that leadeth me.

And when my task on earth is done,
When, by thy grace, the vict'ry's won,
E'en death's cold wave I will not flee,
Since God through Jordan leadeth me.

At the Heart of the Hymn

Joni Eareckson Tada

Teach me to do your will, for you are my God; may your good Spirit lead me on level ground.

—Psalm 143:10

"But, Daddy, do you have to?" I would whine.

That was my typical response on any given Saturday morning back in the fifties when Daddy would take us horseback riding. My father would put aside all his farm duties to saddle up and take us along the trails of the state park bordering our property. My three older sisters were able to bridle and tighten the girths on their own horses, but I was too young to do that. Daddy would swing my little saddle on top of Thunder, cinch her up tight, and then lift me onto her back. I'd gather my reins, and he would adjust my boots in the stirrups. But then he did the dreaded thing. He snapped the lead line on Thunder's bit.

"Please, Daddy, I don't need the lead line! I can steer Thunder by myself!" My father refused to listen to his five-year-old on top of her sixteen-hands-high horse, even if that horse *was* an old gray mare.

So down the trail we ambled, my father in the lead and me, well . . . tethered to him by a long leather lead wrapped around his saddle horn. It was embarrassing. Unlike my sisters bringing up the rear, I couldn't lag back and then race to catch up. I couldn't trot up a side trail to see where it led. I couldn't have the kind of fun they were having. Independence. Freedom to explore. Power to rein in this or that direction. I fumed and folded my arms while Thunder *clip-clopped* slowly along behind my father's horse. What good did reins do me? I couldn't use them anyway.

Finally the day came when Daddy paused for a minute before we left the stable, scratched his head, and then told me I could ride without the lead line.

"Wow! Really?" I had won my independence from having to be second in line. I was no longer tethered to Daddy, and I could kick and steer to my heart's content. I was grown up. Independent. Ready for adventure.

My enthusiasm fizzled, however, when the trail reached the rushing waters of a small river. "Follow me closely," my daddy warned. "I'll show you where it's safe and shallow." He nudged his horse into the swiftly moving current. Thunder flicked her ears and balked, turning her head to sniff my stirrup as though wondering, *Can I trust the kid with this?* I flailed the reins and clucked, hoping she'd find her own footing. Or at least keep up with Daddy's horse.

When we got to the middle of the river, Thunder put her head down to drink. My sisters splashed past, leaving me wet and worried that I would not be able to pull Thunder's head up. The old mare finished drinking and began clopping through the water—but not in the wake of the others. I panicked and dropped the reins in order to wrap both hands around the horn. "Daddy, help!" I cried. The next minute my father was back down the riverbank and cantering toward me in a spray of water. He grabbed Thunder's reins just before she started to wander into the deep part. "Oh, thank you, Daddy, thank you," I kept saying.

My father reached into his saddlebag for the lead line. I was so relieved when he snapped it on Thunder's bit. I was back to being tethered, but it no longer mattered that I couldn't run hither and yon. I was *safe*. Daddy was in front of me, and we were bound together by the lead line.

I sometimes wish I were still on that lead line.

Then again, I am. It's called faith. Faith is the invisible line between me and the Father. You may not see it as you would a real lead line, but it's there. "Now faith is being . . . certain of what we do not see" (Hebrews 1:11). Plus, it's a gift from the Father (Romans 12:3). This is why I pray, *Oh, please, God, put me on the lead line. Increase the measure of my faith. I don't want to go trotting off into trouble, and I realize there's nothing safe about deciding things on my own. There's no safety in lagging behind or running down some side trail in pursuit of my own pleasures. I want to stay hot on Your heels.*

There may be times you will say, "Lord, I can steer by myself." Don't believe it! It's dangerous out there in the current of today's culture.

Take advice from the little kid on the big horse: Stay tethered to your loving Father.

In the Light of the Word

John MacArthur

This beloved song is a tender expression of praise and celebration of the goodness of divine providence. Its opening words are borrowed from the second and third verses of the Twenty-Third Psalm in the King James Version: "He maketh me to lie down in green pastures: *he leadeth me* beside the still waters. He restoreth my soul: *he leadeth me* in the paths of righteousness for his name's sake" (emphasis added).

Scripture is filled with verses that celebrate God's leadership. In Psalm 5:8 the psalmist prays, "Lead me, O Lord, in your righteousness because of my enemies—make straight your way before me." In Isaiah 48:17 God Himself says, "I am the Lord your God, who teaches you what is best for you, who directs you in the way you should go."

God's guidance is always gracious and trustworthy. He says, "I will lead the blind by ways they have not known, along unfamiliar paths I will guide them; I will turn the darkness into light before them and make the rough places smooth. These are the things I will do; I will not forsake them" (Isaiah 42:16).

He guides us, first and foremost, by His Word: "Your word is a lamp to my feet and a light for my path" (Psalm 119:105; cf. verse 133). His Word reveals to us the way we should go.

But more than that, He providentially directs our steps: "He will not let your foot slip—he who watches over you will not slumber. . . . The Lord will keep you from all harm—he will watch over your life; the LORD will watch over your coming and going both now and forevermore" (Psalm 121:3, 7-8). "In his heart a man plans his course, but the LORD determines his steps" (Proverbs 16:9).

God providentially governs even the smallest details of our lives. That was Jesus' point in Matthew 10:29-30, when He said that not one sparrow falls to the ground apart from the will of God. The very hairs on our heads are all numbered. In other words, nothing in life is so insignificant that God is unconcerned or uninvolved in it. He sovereignly orchestrates His providence so that "all things" work together for our good (Romans 8:28).

That is indeed a "blessed thought," filled to the brim (or "fraught") with "heav'nly comfort."

The song celebrates the sovereignty of divine providence that superintends every moment of our lives without exception: "Whate'er I do, where'er I be, still 'tis God's hand that leadeth me." David said the same thing in Psalm 139:7-10:

Where can I go from your Spirit?
Where can I flee from your presence?
If I go up to the heavens, you are there;
if I make my bed in the depths, you are there.
If I rise on the wings of the dawn,
if I settle on the far side of the sea,
even there your hand will guide me,
your right hand will hold me fast.

Stanza 2 of the hymn makes a similar series of contrasts. God guides us "'mid scenes of deepest gloom" as well as in the most Edenic environments. His hand leads whether He takes us "by waters calm, [or] o'er troubled sea." Whether we sense His presence or not, Scripture promises that He is governing all our steps (Proverbs 20:24). And to believers, Scripture makes this promise: "If the LORD delights in a man's way, he makes his steps firm; though he stumble, he will not fall, for the Lord upholds him with his hand" (Psalm 37:23-24).

Stanza 3 is a prayer of consecration and absolute trust in the goodness of divine providence no matter what. The one who understands God's sovereign care need never "murmur nor repine." Because we know that the One who is leading and ordering our steps is working all things for our good, we may be "content, whatever lot [we] see."

The closing stanza carries the thought to the very end of life, "when my task on earth is done." Death, though our enemy (1 Corinthians 15:26), has already been conquered by Christ; so we can follow Him confidently even there. This too echoes the Twenty-Third Psalm: "Even though I walk through the valley of the shadow of death, I will fear no evil, for you are with me; your rod and your staff, they comfort me" (v. 4).

From Out of the Past

Bobbie Wolgemuth

America was reeling from the devastation of the Civil War in the 1860s. Soldiers and civilians were turning to God, and singing as spiritual revival was sweeping the land. In the city of Philadelphia, a visiting preacher named Joseph Gilmore was holding two weeks of meetings at the First Baptist Church. "The City of Brotherly Love" had been experiencing a reawakening with crowded noonday meetings held under the direction of the YMCA. God was at work, and Dr. Gilmore knew it.

Joseph Gilmore was more than just a preacher. He was a scholar, editor, composer, and college professor of Hebrew, logic, rhetoric, and English literature. With all the scholarship, however, Joseph was sensitive to God's voice when a thought kept repeating itself in his mind. Such was the case on a Wednesday evening when he wrote the words to "He Leadeth Me."

After his midweek speaking engagement, one thought from the text of his evening sermon kept begging for a simple explanation. How could he make the Twenty-third Psalm relevant to the people who needed comfort and inspiration while they grieved the hatred and sorrow brought on by the war? Does God really guide through the valleys and the shadows of death? The twenty-eight-year-old preacher and his young wife walked next door to a deacon's home for some lively discussion after the service. While pondering the notion of God's leading, he quickly wrote several verses on a piece of paper and handed it to his wife. That was the last he remembered of it until several years later.

Unknown to Joseph, his wife sent the poem he had scribbled to a Boston paper called *The Watchman and Reflector*. It was just a short time until it was discovered. Drawn to its memorable lines and simple thought, a leading composer of the day found it and decided to set it to music. William Bradbury, who had written a number of Sunday school melodies including "Jesus Loves Me" and "Just As I Am," found just the right tune for the shepherd verse. Completing it by adding the lines to the chorus, "His faithful follower I would be, for by his hand he leadeth me," he put it into a new hymnal.

Three years later Joseph Gilmore went to preach as a candidate for the Second Baptist Church in Rochester, New York. He picked up a hymnbook in the chapel, wondering what kind of songs they used at that church. The page fell open to "He Leadeth Me." It was the first time he knew his verse had found a place among the songs of the church. He never disclosed whether or not that was the reason he took the pastorate of that church for two years! He did say that he would never forget the impression it made on him to come in contact with his own assertion of "God's blessed leadership."

Later the hymn was translated into many different languages. Although written during the Civil War era, it spanned the gap to another war in American history. Military men during World War II heard it being sung in the South Pacific by native people. The hymn was one that continued to be a great surprise.

WORDS AND MUSIC

Lead On, O King Eternal

Ernest W. Shurtleff, 1888

LANCASHIRE 7.6.7.6.D.
Henry Smart, 1836

My Jesus, I Love Thee

William R. Featherstone, 1864

CARITAS 11.11.11.11.
Adoniram J. Gordon, 1894

How Firm a Foundation

5. "E'en down to old age all my people shall prove
my sovereign, eternal, unchangeable love;
and when hoary hairs shall their temples adorn,
like lambs they shall still in my bosom be borne.

6. "The soul that on Jesus has leaned for repose,
I will not, I will not desert to his foes;
that soul, though all hell should endeavor to shake,
I'll never, no never, no never forsake."

Rippon's *Selection of Hymns*, 1787; alt.
Mod.

FOUNDATION 11.11.11.11.
Traditional American melody
J. Funk's *A Compilation of Genuine Church Music*, 1832

Amazing Grace!

5. And when this flesh and heart shall fail,
   and mortal life shall cease,
   I shall possess within the veil
   a life of joy and peace.

6. When we've been there ten thousand years,
   bright shining as the sun,
   we've no less days to sing God's praise
   than when we've first begun.

St. 1–5, John Newton, 1779
St. 6, *A Collection of Sacred Ballads*, 1790

AMAZING GRACE C.M.
Traditional American melody
Arr. by Edwin O. Excell, 1900

When Morning Gilds the Skies

5. Let earth's wide circle round
in joyful notes resound:
May Jesus Christ be praised.
Let air and sea and sky,
from depth to height, reply:
May Jesus Christ be praised.

6. Be this, while life is mine,
my canticle divine:
May Jesus Christ be praised.
Be this th'eternal song,
through all the ages on:
May Jesus Christ be praised.

German, ca. 1800
Tr. by Edward Caswall, 1853, 1858

LAUDES DOMINI 6.6.6.D.
Joseph Barnby, 1868

Guide Me, O Thou Great Jehovah

William Williams, 1745
St. 1 tr. by Peter Williams, 1771
St. 2–3 tr. by William Williams, 1772

CWM RHONDDA 8.7.8.7.8.7. rep.
John Hughes, 1907

Love Divine, All Loves Excelling

Charles Wesley, 1747

BEECHER 8.7.8.7.D.
John Zundel, 1870; alt. 1990

More Love to Thee, O Christ

Elizabeth Payson Prentiss, 1869

MORE LOVE TO THEE 6.4.6.4.6.6.4.4.
William H. Doane, 1868

All the Way My Savior Leads Me

Fanny J. Crosby, 1875

ALL THE WAY 8.7.8.7.D.
Robert Lowry, 1875; alt. 1990

Holy, Holy, Holy!

Reginald Heber, 1783-1826

NICAEA 11.12.12.10.
John B. Dykes, 1861

When He Cometh, When He Cometh

William O. Cushing, 1823-1903

JEWELS 8.6.8.5.ref.
George Frederick Root, 1820-1895

He Leadeth Me: O Blessed Thought!

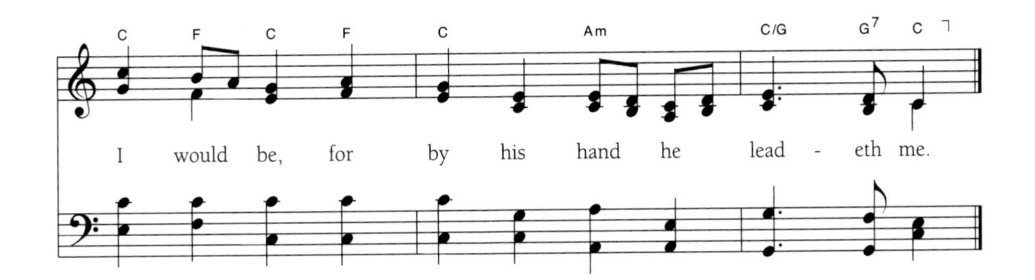

Joseph H. Gilmore, 1862; alt.

HE LEADETH ME L.M.D.
William B. Bradbury, 1864